Archi tecture and Climate Change

Vol. 1

Sandra Hofmeister
Ed.

Contents

Circular and CO_2-neutral

Resources and Reserves

When Will the Construction Turnaround Come?

In many parts of the world today, climate change presents a dire threat to human lives and livelihoods. The pace of global warming is increasing, with rising sea levels and floods, prolonged droughts, failed harvests, and famine escalating year by year. This urgency drove the United Nations to establish the Paris Climate Agreement in 2015, with the aim of capping global warming at 1.5 degrees Celsius above pre-industrial levels. However, achieving significant reductions in greenhouse gases is not possible without a fundamental paradigm shift. Our disposable society must become a circular one.

One key to achieving this transformation is prioritizing the reuse of raw materials over depleting extraction practices. Industrialized nations undoubtedly carry a significant responsibility in leading the transition toward a more sustainable future and must actively engage in fulfilling this duty. With the European Green Deal, the European Union has committed to achieving zero net greenhouse gas emissions by the year 2050. The roadmap to achieving carbon neutrality is now clearly defined, with specific, legally binding steps laid out in the EU Taxonomy. The reality of the climate emergency is widely recognized, with a consensus that immediate action is essential. However, as we approach nearly a decade since the Paris Agreement, where do we currently stand?

2024 had the warmest January ever recorded globally – temperatures are rising faster than expected. In 2023, average temperatures exceeded pre-industrial levels by 1.52 degrees Celsius, surpassing the UN target for the first time. Does this trend suggest that achieving climate neutrality is slipping beyond our grasp? How can we prevent crossing the irreversible tipping point towards a catastrophic global climate crisis? In response to this new data, the European Commission has revised its targets, aiming for swifter reductions in greenhouse gas emissions. While the goals are becoming more ambitious,

Sandra Hofmeister

can their implementation keep pace with reality? Moreover, what role does the construction industry play in confronting these challenges?

With around 40 % of global carbon emissions stemming from the construction sector, a sustainable turnaround in construction is imperative for any meaningful progress in tackling climate change. Taking Germany as an example, data from the German Federal Environment Agency reveals that the construction industry consumes over 70 % of all raw materials mined in the country, despite the finite nature of these resources. Simultaneously, this sector is responsible for 54 % of the nation's waste. This stark imbalance underscores the dilemma at hand. Architecture must transform radically, as must our understanding of it. New ideas and ideals are required, as the conventional architectural parameters have become outdated. Fortunately, promising concepts are beginning to emerge.

Navigating the complexities of climate change, this book considers the goals and demands placed on architecture within this context and highlights the potential contributions of the discipline towards achieving climate neutrality. Technical details such as building insulation standards, energy-saving regulations, or CO_2 calculations are not the primary focus. Rather, our interviews with international experts emphasize human realities and the associated architectural needs. We delve into how climate change affects living conditions and daily life across various regions, cities, and continents. Architects, urban planners, and landscape designers share their experiences, articulate their convictions, and outline actionable scenarios. This book showcases diverse perspectives addressing climate change politically, socially, economically, and ecologically.

What can architecture do to mitigate the catastrophic consequences of climate change? Practical solutions include emergency shelters for those displaced by flooding or floating schools in flood-prone areas – as explored in our conversations with the Japanese Pritzker Prize winner Shigeru Ban and the Nigerian architect Kunlé Adeyemi. Discussions with architects Tatiana Bilbao and Marina Tabassum highlight the stark climate realities faced in Mexico and Bangladesh. Copenhagen's city architect Camilla van Deurs unpacks the policies propelling the Danish capital towards climate neutrality, while Singapore-based architect and urban planner Richard Hassell shares his vision for developing the city-state as a model green city. In addition to the regional and geographical focal points covered in the first part of the book, the chapter titled "Circular and CO_2-ncutral" cxamincs innovativc construction methods, with European perspectives providing concrete circular solutions. Michael Braungart, who pioneered the cradle-to-cradle principle many years ago, takes a critical look at the achievements we can boast today. Anders Lendager from Denmark and Swiss architect Barbara Buser are two experienced planners who share their experiences with circular construction. The final chapter of this book investigates what other resources and reserves are available to further the transformation of construction practices. In addition to natural, CO_2-neutral materials like straw, clay, or wood, existing building stock is one of the most important repositories of raw materials – yet its potential often remains untapped.

When will construction turn the corner on sustainability? It's understandable that no one can give a definite answer to this complex question, and we certainly can't expect the interviewees in this book to predict the future. However, our conversations demonstrate the tangible progress being made by the industry towards a more sustainable future. Now, the challenge lies in accelerating these efforts to match the urgency of climate change.

Sandra Hofmeister

Cities and Regions

Chapter 1

Building Respon sibly

Interview
Marina Tabassum

With her projects in Bangladesh, Marina Tabassum supports those particularly affected by climate change. In this interview with Vera Simone Bader, the architect from Dhaka describes the challenges she faces.

Much of Bangladesh is below sea level, and the water is rising. The increase in severe flooding caused by climate change has wreaked havoc in parts of the country. An estimated 7.2 million people were affected in 2022 alone. What can architecture do to counter this growing threat?

There are many challenges associated with the climate crisis, such as economic disparity and inequity, marginalization, imbalance in the ecosystem and environment, and increasing stockpiles of waste, only to name a few. All these challenges call for innovative methods in architecture that requires critical engagement with people and place. This certainly cannot only be about focusing on the production of a building. We should look beyond the object and consider creativity as a problem-solving act. To do this, we need to expand our skills as architects and create projects with people and then arrange funding or patronage. It's a matter of being present physically and working closely with the community to resolve the challenges. This means that we will have to rethink the role of the architect and, with it, the agendas of the profession.

What is the responsibility of architects in these times of climate insecurity?

Build responsibly: this responsibility begins with the question of whether we need to build at all or whether we reuse existing structures. Source responsibly: we need to focus on reducing long supply chains and source locally as much as possible. Design responsibly: to reduce our dependency on mechanical means of operation and maintenance.

Marina Tabassum

You mentioned the need for new methods in architecture; what approaches do you take in your search for innovative and appropriate solutions?

For us, research is fundamental to understanding where the problems are. For example, we study the geographical location that is affected by the changes in climate. The coastal region of Bangladesh, for example, has always possessed landscape dynamics evoked by water. With the prolonged rains caused by the climate crisis and the foreshortened glacial water flowing down from the Himalayas, we face entirely new challenges. It was important for us to find out how this situation was affecting people. So, we had to be on the ground to understand the impact and how it affects human lives. Only then could we find actual solutions that would be practical and relevant. Intervention in vernacular living that can sustain and be adopted by the people takes a long time.

Can you give an example of how you have developed a solution based on your research?

For a project on the coast of Bangladesh, we were influenced by the local construction methods. Particularly along the rivers, the local population builds houses in a timber frame knock-down construction. These houses are a flourishing business in Dohar, Lohajang, and Munshiganj. We took the idea of the knock-down system and developed a low-cost space frame structure that can be moved from one place to another. We call this system Khudi Bari. The cost-effectiveness makes it affordable for people who have lost their land to erosion and have no means of income. The people who live along the riverbanks of Bangladesh are a marginalized group. Our structure is therefore made of bamboo, a natural and inexpensive material, and steel for the connections to facilitate mobility. It is divided into two levels of liveable space so the residents can move higher to the upper level if flood waters rise too fast, for example. This simple system is scalable and has the potential to respond to very different problems.

“Responsibility begins with the question of whether we need to build at all or whether we reuse existing structures.”

Marina Tabassum

Khudi Bari (tiny house) are low-cost, mobile bamboo homes designed for resilience during flooding, by Marina Tabassum Architects.

You touched on it before, but what can architects learn from the local population, who have always lived with the water, monsoons, and flooding?

The people who are affected the most by the climate crisis have a zero carbon footprint. They take an inherently sustainable approach to housing construction by using materials they can find in their immediate landscape. They grow their own food and have no dependency on electricity or running water. In general, vernacular architecture always responds to the climate. This type of construction never strives to be unusual or flashy, but continues to evolve and be perfected from generation to generation. These are important lessons that an architect can learn and practice in many ways.

You have designed structures with bamboo and clay, but they have always been located outside of the megacity of Dhaka. How can cities be persuaded to embrace a new approach to urban architecture?

The values that come from vernacular construction are transferable everywhere. You can think locally in any area, both in terms of materials and labour. Craftspeople and artisans stimulate the local economy; that's not to be underestimated. However, I think we need to question the city itself. In the past, there were good reasons why we needed cities: industrialization and the associated ecology of that time. With the fast development of communication technologies, our physical presence can be replaced by virtual connectivity; our geographical presence has become secondary. I can live a quality life in a village if my basic needs, such as education, health, and a proper living environment, are met. So we should focus more on liveability in rural areas and small towns to reduce the pressure on our metropolitan areas. That will make us all healthier. We can then build with natural materials in the smaller towns. Only when we rethink the city can we really make a difference there.

Vernacular construction: The timber frame structure of this typical prefabricated house, developed by residents of the Ganges-Brahmaputra river basin, is available for purchase at local markets in Lohajang, Munshiganj, and Dohar.

“We should focus more on liveability in rural areas and small towns to reduce the pressure on our metropolitan areas.”

Marina Tabassum

Climate Change as a Social Issue

Interview
Tatiana Bilbao

For Tatiana Bilbao from Mexico City, diversity and a culture of care are needed to combat the climate crisis. In conversation with Sandra Hofmeister, she describes how architecture can help.

For its general water supply, Mexico City pumps water over long distances into the urban area. But increasing droughts and climate change are causing supply shortages, and water is becoming an ever more precious resource. Are you an optimist or a pessimist, when it comes to the future of the city?

Mexico City will definitively stay. But I don't know if we humans are going to survive in the city. Since the 1970s when it was created, the Cutzamala water supply system has pumped water from as far as the state of Hidalgo, through the mountains and into the valley of Mexico City. We are relying on other parts of the country for this basic need. Considering that Mexico City is built on a lake, the situation becomes even more crazy. For the Aztecs who once settled on its shore, it was essential for survival. But then the Spanish arrived with their own idea of how cities should be. For 300 years, they did everything they could to drain the lake. Even today in Mexico City we are living on its muddied bed, which creates major problems. We are not allowing water to infiltrate the ground, and therefore the city is sinking. We urgently need a solution for how to continue living in Mexico City. The answer is not pumping water from more distant regions until those areas go dry as well.

So it's about changing how the situation is addressed in general?

We need to change society in a way that enables us to work together and understand each other. For me, fundamental social transformation is crucial for the future. We must transform our society, from a set of relationships based on productivity and monetary exchange to a culture of care – for each other and for everything that surrounds us. For this to happen, we need to radically transform our relationship to people and things.

Where do we start?

So far, we have been wasteful with resources. We have to consume them more wisely, distribute them more fairly, and take social responsibility. I don't think we need to invent new things. We can use what already exists – but we have to use them more sensibly and responsibly.

In 1972, the Club of Rome pointed out that economic growth was limited by the Earth's finite natural resources. How can we change this system focused on growth and production?

In order to exist, we need to produce; there is no other way. But we do not need new products for the existential aspects of our life on this planet. We need to put our energy into supporting each other. I agree with economist Mariana Mazzucato, who believes we need a new narrative of wealth that is no longer based on more production, consumption, and expansion. Architecture can do a lot to support this new way of thinking, focused on care. So far, there are not many spaces, places, or cities built around social transformation for the better. So let's build them!

How can a major industry such as construction detach itself from the principle of profit?

There is an existential necessity to do so, and we need to recognize this necessity in order to become a more sustainable society. It also involves fundamentally questioning how

“A culture of care, for each other and for everything around us, should be at the heart of society.”

Tatiana Bilbao

Design collages by Tatjana Bilbao for the Mazatlán Aquarium in the Mexican state of Sinaloa.

buildings are constructed. We should think in much more local terms overall, and return to respecting the environment, instead of trying to dominate it. The construction industry often operates according to egocentric and unsustainable principles. This includes the belief in universal solutions that can be applied to building projects everywhere. But it's obvious that solutions cannot at all be universal!

Can you give me an example?

For the last 16 years, we having been working on projects at the Culiacán Botanical Garden in Sinaloa state. The average temperature there is 30 °C, and in the summer it can get up to 50 °C. With global warming, it will be even worse. Given those circumstances, of course we cannot build with wood. So we use bricks and concrete – it's the right choice for the region. Wood construction in general does not work in Mexico due to the climate.

So it's also about material diversity?

Just like our climate regions and social structures, each of us is different. Recognizing this diversity is, in my opinion, the central paradigm of the 21st century. The paradigm of the 20th century was equality and democracy – although we have not achieved that. Right now what we really need to do is accept that we each have our own differences.

Your designs often take up the idea of understanding nature. What can we learn from nature?

I used to think of nature as something that surrounds us. But at some point, I realized that this concept was much too limited. We can only change the future for the better if we realize that we are also part of nature. Until now, we have believed that we can organize our daily lives independently of nature, in climate-controlled and artificially lit buildings. But this alienated us from the fact that we ourselves are part of the system of nature. We need to re-learn to accept the natural fluctuations of outdoor temperatures and sunlight. Of course, we can also control the situation for a certain degree of comfort, but we should not be completely alienated from nature.

Where are we today in this process of growing closer to nature?

Europe already has many pioneering approaches. But in the US, many spaces are 18 °C the whole year round and the lights are on, no matter what time of the day or night. That is a serious mistake. Why don't we allow it to be warm in the summer and colder in the winter, or sleep when it's dark outside? Architecture can create spaces that foster this understanding.

It is easier for the wealthy to give up a few privileges. But what are the prospects for poorer regions and countries?

We have forgotten that the privileges of the rich come at the expense of the rights of poor people. In fact, the poor often take an exemplary attitude toward others. They often understand the necessity of relying on nature much more than we do.

The aquarium's open concrete architecture aims to make the ecosystem of the Sea of Cortez and its coastal regions into a tangible experience.

Tatiana Bilbao

Design sketch and collages for the Mazatlán Aquarium.

“We can only change the future for the better if we realize that we are also part of nature.”

Tatiana Bilbao

Testing Ground to Save the World

Interview
Tarik Oualalou

African countries are suffering the most from the impacts of global climate change. Architect Tarik Oualalou, based in Casablanca and Paris, tells Jakob Schoof that the continent represents our last opportunity to test improved urbanization models.

You recently argued that Africa needs to reinvent its cities, and that people there need to relearn nomadic living. Why is that?

Today, 3.5 billion people live in cities around the world. In 20 years, it will be 6.5 billion. This means that in two decades we will have three billion new urban dwellers – half of them in Africa alone. We would have to build a new city for 1.5 million people every week on the continent! That kind of growth is unfathomable, and our existing urban structures are not designed for it at all. Large parts of Africa will become uninhabitable over the next few decades, including areas where cities are located today. We will experience a transition period in which cities will cease to exist, causing huge waves of migration, and new cities will have to be built at a rapid pace. So far, the only solution we have to this situation is the United Nations refugee camps, which are based on a post-World War II model. They are hardly suitable for contemporary city dwellers. It's time we architects took up the cause. We need to take the urban visions of Archigram and others from the late 20th century and make them buildable. And we need to see what we can learn from the nomadic lifestyles of previous generations. I'm thinking of buildings that can be put up and taken down quickly, and infrastructure that is no longer dug into the ground. Temporary settlements that still offer everything a city needs: markets, public spaces, and the cultivation and processing of food on site.

What does your vision mean for existing cities?

Tarik Oualalou

I am not calling to wipe out our existing cities, but to take stock of a new reality whose consequences we have not thought about seriously enough. Megacities have a fundamental problem: they depend on supply networks of a size that proves unsustainable in times of crisis. Just think of the constant water shortages in the Los Angeles region, and the conflicts there between urban and rural populations over water resources. Now imagine this situation in a city like Lagos, which has far fewer financial resources. In the future, we will have to reduce cities and their infrastructures to a manageable size. This would help to avoid transregional conflicts over resources, and would also make the infrastructure easier to manage. While state governments in Africa often have little legitimacy, city governments generally function well, and mayors are highly respected.

Africa is often viewed somewhat one-sidedly as a victim of climate change. What resources does it have to cope with global warming?

Africa today is effectively a testing ground for the rest of humanity. It is the last continent to be caught up in the global wave of urbanization. In this respect, it is also our last chance to meet this challenge better than in other parts of the world. In Europe, I can choose whether to be wasteful with energy or to use it sparingly and whether or not to let the water run in the bathroom. You can't do that in Africa – the consequences would be immediate. Sustainability is vital to life there. No city in Africa can survive without clever energy management and the economical use of water.

Where do you see efforts moving in the right direction?

Africa is a mosaic of different countries and traditions. The situation in Egypt or Morocco is entirely different from that in Nigeria, South Africa, or Kenya. But there are three basic

Redevelopment plan by Oualalou + Choi for the
Ain Sebaa corniche in Casablanca.

Tarik Oualalou

currents that I see underway on the continent. First, decentralized initiatives and individual experiments are often much more powerful than state reforms imposed from above. Second, African societies are strongly characterized by rituals and collective thinking; the belief that there is something more important than my own private ego is, in my opinion, one of the continent's most valuable resources. And third, the relationship with the industrialized North, specifically Europe, is currently turning around: we are experiencing a moment of decolonization, in which people are less and less willing to blindly adopt models of the Global North, but are instead working on viable local solutions. Taken together, these three currents could form the foundation on which we can build a collective future for our continent.

“People in Africa are less and less willing to blindly adopt models of the Global North.”

Tarik Oualalou

Living with Water

Interview
Kunlé Adeyemi

How can coastal cities adapt to rising sea levels? In conversation with Heide Wessely, Nigerian architect Kunlé Adeyemi discusses solutions to climate change.

Sea levels are rising. Can architecture influence climate change, or can architects only react to its effects?

Architects and planners can play a huge role in climate change as we think about the built environment and how to design for the future. But that question should have been asked and answered 20 years ago. Unfortunately, we are now on quite a steep trajectory with the impacts of climate change. That's why we should not only think about changing the built environment but also adapting to the changing natural environment. In terms of rising sea levels, we must learn to live with water instead of trying to fight it.

In which ways?

We could build on the water on floating structures or stilts. Many indigenous communities have lived on and around water for millennia, especially in Africa and Asia – the continents most affected by climate change today. We are working to understand how these communities live with water and to develop that into a new way of living. There are countless settlements built around and on the water that work well. The easiest solution is to learn from them. We also need to reduce our reliance on concrete and use nature-based building materials instead, like wood, bamboo, and stone. They are great materials that are used where they grow. It doesn't make sense to transport building materials around the world.

How can modern cities learn from indigenous settlements?

The Floating Music Hub by Kunlé Adeyemi is a space for music and cultural events made of prefabricated timber elements. It is anchored in Mindelo, Cape Verde.

We need to allow more water into the urban fabric of our cities and create waterways. In April of 2022, hundreds of people died from the floods in Durban, South Africa. I studied the city with my students at Harvard a few years ago, and even then, we saw that flood mitigation measures were lacking. Solutions exist, but they have yet to be developed. First, we need a change of mindset; 80 % of our major cities and capitals around the world are located on a waterfront. Many of them, especially in developing countries, are growing very fast. Those are two major challenges: rapid urbanization and climate change. If we look at water as a new property to be developed, we could build entire water cities.

You grew up in Lagos and have long lived in Amsterdam. Don't these very different societies and cultures need different solutions?

Yes, in Nigeria, the reality is very different from that in the Netherlands; Lagos alone has more people than all of the Netherlands. The challenges and how they are dealt with are inherently very different. In Nigeria, there is a strong awareness of the immediate impact that human actions have; social responsibility is deeply ingrained in the African context. In the Netherlands, a strong awareness of environmental sustainability has led to new technologies. Combining these two approaches would be very valuable. A sense of social responsibility would benefit many parts of the West, and Western technologies would be helpful to many African cities.

What do you think about knowledge sharing between Africa and the Western world?

I definitely think an exchange of ideas can be beneficial, but it is not as straightforward as simply taking an idea and applying it to another context. Solutions must be relevant to the particular situation and should mostly be homegrown. One place with close parallels to the Netherlands is Makoko, a vast informal settlement mainly built on stilts in the Lagos Lagoon. The urban fabric of Amsterdam already has a great deal of water, but there are still plenty of opportunities to increase real estate by creating more infrastructure directly on water as opposed to the costly practice of land reclamation. The Netherlands has technologies, knowledge, and resources to solve problems like waste management, sewage, and power. But the Dutch could still learn a lot from the inhabitants of Makoko about embracing water as a way of life.

Your floating school prototype in Lagos has evolved into the Makoko Floating System. How does it work, and where is it being built?

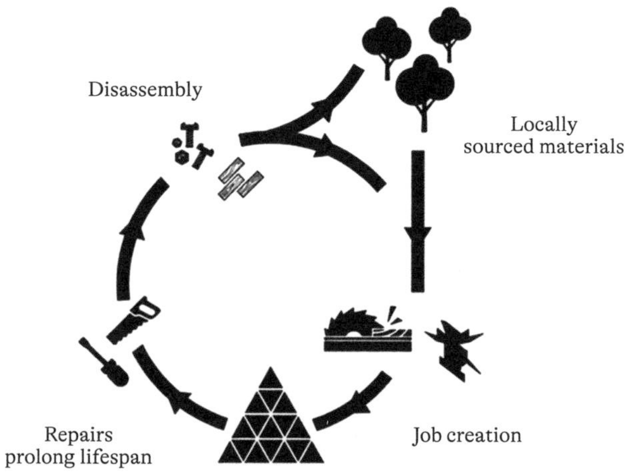

"We need to let water into our cities, not fight against it."

Kunlé Adeyemi

Unlike stilt structures, our floating platform prototype adapts to the changing tide levels. We also wanted to create a system that a family or community could build on its own. That is why we used small timber elements that can be easily assembled by hand. They can be used to create buildings with up to three floors – that's quite tall for a floating structure. The construction is very basic and can be built with wood or bamboo by unskilled workers. Poorer populations all over the world can use it to build floating houses. The school in Makoko was an innovation. We built it with the community, saw it in operation, saw it get damaged, and saw it collapse after a storm. We learned a lot from it; sometimes, things must fail before they succeed. Since then, we have built five floating buildings on three continents and adapted them to the given water, climate, and environmental conditions. Right now, I'm in Cape Verde, where we combined three floating units into a centre for music and culture with state-of-the-art technical equipment. Our system can serve a wide variety of functions: housing, healthcare, culture, or administration.

Makoko is a settlement built on the waters of the Lagos lagoon. The floating school, designed for the community by Kunlé Adeyemi and his architecture firm NLÉ, was in operation for three years.

Kunlé Adeyemi

Copenhagen's Climate Neutral Path

Interview
Camilla van Deurs

Camilla van Deurs is the Chief City Architect of the Danish capital. She sees the potential in architecture and urban planning to drastically sink CO_2 emissions and improve quality of life. She explains to Sandra Hofmeister how this can be done.

What are your tasks as Chief City Architect of Copenhagen?

I am an advisor to the politicians and to the administration, meaning that I see and touch almost everything that is built in the city. The question of climate neutrality is increasingly important in this regard. About 30 % of the CO_2 emissions in Copenhagen are related to the building industry and about 30 % are related to mobility. To me, mobility is also part of architecture and city planning. Building metro stations, cycle lanes, and car-free zones in the city centre are very much about reducing the climate impact.

The city's ambition is to become carbon neutral as soon as possible. What does this mean in terms of urban planning?

All new city districts will be built along the metro lines. Aside from that, we always include "soft mobility", such as bicycles and bicycle lanes, in our planning. Also the new city districts will be integrated into the existing urban fabric. That means we must think about bicycle bridges, tunnels, new intersections, and ways to connect the new neighbourhoods to the rest of the city when it comes to urban planning. This vital task is often overlooked because architects and planners focus on their projects, although linking to the city is probably the most interesting aspect. Last but not least, all new city districts will be either car-free or planned as very low car ownership districts. In practice, we have reduced car parking to one per approximately four households.

Copenhagen will be 86 % climate-neutral by 2025 – a success rooted in a long-term strategy.

Cyclists are privileged compared to car owners in Copenhagen. What are the next steps of your cycling strategy?

The history of cycling in Copenhagen stems from the energy crisis in 1973. But there is a constant discussion about it. Today we have come to the point where about 50 % of Copenhageners use a bike to commute, either by cycling to a station and then taking the metro or cycling all the way to work and school. One of our next steps is to reduce car parking spaces in the central city, which creates a conflict, of course.

How are you dealing with this conflict?

There are 126,000 public parking spaces today on the streets of Copenhagen. Altogether, that is a two-and-a-half times bigger surface than our biggest public park. If we reduce parking spaces, we can create greener streets with room for trees, children, and people to walk and cycle. Our narrative is not about what we are losing, but what each of us is gaining. Of course, we do not have a magic button to solve the car parking question, but we've tried a few projects and adopted the Citizens' Assembly methodology from Toronto. It is a democratic election of citizens who convene to discuss the topic and then give recommendations to politicians. Based on their recommendation, the city of Copenhagen has decided to remove close to 85 % of surface parking in the historic centre. I think politicians dare to take this decision because citizens have chosen this as the direction to go. In the summer of 2021, we also conducted a series of experiments where we closed five streets for some months, set out planters and benches, and then evaluated the public response. Generally, a good way to deal with sustainability issues is to try out different concepts and count on the democratic dialogue.

Since 2009, the city has already reduced CO_2 emissions by 68 % – a huge success. Yet the ambitious deadline to become carbon neutral by 2025 still had to be postponed. Why?

The reason for postponing is the CopenHill waste-to-energy plant. To be 100 % carbon neutral, we must have a technical carbon capture facility. But that won't be ready until 2028. So, Copenhagen will be 98 % carbon neutral in 2025, but the final 2 % is yet to come.

Decarbonization often means restrictions. In Copenhagen, you explain it as a method for a better quality of life. CopenHill, for example, is not only a waste-to-energy plant but also has a ski slope on its rooftop. Is that part of your overall strategy?

We can only achieve systemic change by including citizens' behaviour. And to change it, you have to invite people to see it as a benefit in their everyday life. The energy sources and the CopenHill waste-to-energy plant are crucial for our climate strategy; 65 % of our CO_2 decrease is thanks to energy efficiency and energy production. Particularly now, with the war in Ukraine, we all understand how vital energy is. But for Copenhagen, it was initially about having a reliable and sustainable central heating system for all citizens.

Energy and heating systems in Denmark have green sources. Copenhagen is not dependent on Russian gas ...

Indeed: in Copenhagen, energy is 98 % sustainable. It uses wind, sun, garbage incineration, and wood-burning, which is less sustainable. But wood pellets will be phased out in the coming years. It is important for architecture to develop a visual language to reflect green energy, as does the CopenHill by BIG. Citizens understand that their garbage goes to this waste-to-energy plant, where we have a ski slope and biodiversity park on top, which contribute to the city skyline. It is

During rush hour, a "green wave" synchronizes traffic lights for cyclists, facilitating smoother travel.

Camilla van Deurs

crucial to make them see their the garbage doesn't just go to some dump somewhere and disappear.

> In July 2023, as the Unesco World Capital of Architecture, Copenhagen hosted the World Congress of the Union of International Architects. What were your expectations?

We had a full programme, including 17 temporary pavilions built along the harbourfront addressing the question: "How are we building in the future?" Around 50 new architecture projects were launched that year, from schools to swimming pools and new parks. I was glad about the discussions on what we can learn from other cities and countries. We can use this input for the new architecture policy and municipal plan that we are designing. For me personally, the dialogue is the most important, and it offers us a chance. We proudly showcase and share Copenhagen, but we must also be humble and listen to our visitors.

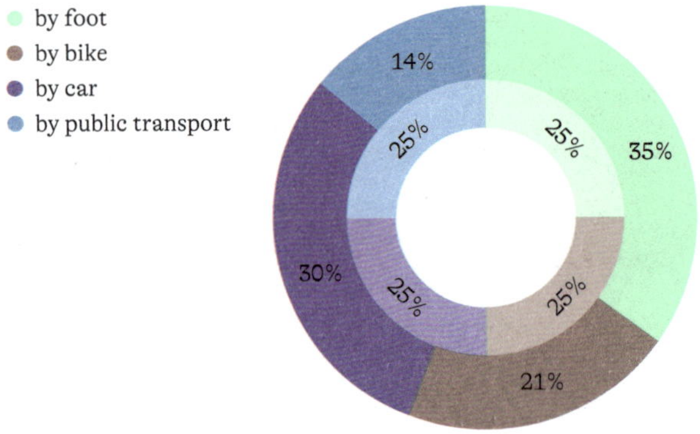

Modal split in Copenhagen: The outer ring shows the status quo in 2021; the inner ring shows the targets for 2025 (source: City of Copenhagen, TUdata).

"It is crucial to make people see that their garbage does not just disappear."

Camilla van Deurs

Climate Shelters for Barcelona

Interview
Lacol

Carles Baiges CB and Eliseu Arrufat EA from Catalan architecture collective Lacol describe to Heide Wessely how the dense city of Barcelona is defying climate change.

Barcelona is one of the most densely populated cities in Europe, with 12,000 inhabitants per square kilometre; only Paris has more. How does a city of this density cope with global warming?

CB The city's density has many advantages in terms of sustainability, but there are also disadvantages. It's positive that less area is sealed overall, plus nearly everything you need for daily life is within walking distance. You don't need a car to go grocery shopping, and even getting to work is possible for many by bike or e-scooter. A major drawback, however, is that the city has too few green spaces, which are essential for healthy living and greater climate resilience. The city government is addressing this issue by establishing superblocks and green axes. "Superblocks" are clusters of low-traffic city blocks within the checkerboard urban grid designed by Ildefons Cerdà in 1860. The "green axes" are streets connecting these superblocks, which will also have reduced traffic and green landscaping.

Can these urban planning measures solve the problem of global warming?

CB They will at least contribute to a healthier life for city residents. At the same time, they are the subject of intense debate because they can lead to gentrification. But what is the alternative? Nothing? Finding the balance is a delicate issue. We must improve the city without worsening the situation for some residents. Socially responsible urban transformation is a topic we frequently address in our work.

How can this succeed? What role does social equity play in creating a more sustainable city?

CB The influence of social class on the success or failure of achieving higher levels of sustainability in the city is significant. People who are struggling financially usually aren't worried about whether their apartment building consumes too much energy. We are currently refurbishing 1970s apartment blocks in a very low-income area on the outskirts of Barcelona. Given today's high energy costs, the buildings urgently need to be more energy efficient. But the residents trust neither the experts nor the government. They often don't see the need to change anything.

EA There is a danger that the climate debate will deepen social divides. The wealthy are better positioned to demand and implement more environmentally sustainable measures in the city. It also doesn't help that permits and funding applications for solar panels are so complicated that they are nearly impossible to complete without help. You have to pay someone to clear the bureaucratic hurdles for a permit. These applications are so complex that you need a university degree to understand them – things like this reinforce class differences.

What is the role of politics in climate-friendly construction?

EA Left-leaning governments make things easier because they focus more on social concerns. But even more important is the pressure exerted by the European Union; we are observing how conservative governments around Spain are going backwards in regard to climate change policies. But the last two extremely hot and dry summers here in Barcelona, as well as the drought we are experiencing right now, have accelerated a change in thinking. People are feeling climate change firsthand. High energy costs also play their part.

"The influence of social class in achieving higher levels of sustainability is significant."

Lacol

Lacol has its office at La Comunal, Lacol is headquartered at La Comunal, a former industrial site in Barcelona's Sants neighbourhood that the architects renovated and expanded into a cultural quarter.

What kind of framework would enable you to build in a more climate-friendly way?

CB Building regulations in Barcelona are highly restrictive. Too many representatives from different administrations have a say in a project, and anyone can object and reject proposals. Deviating from regulations in a sustainable, climate-friendly way is possible, but not without intensive negotiations. We have tried to do that with our projects, to considerable success. For example, for the La Borda cooperative housing project, we managed to avoid having to build an underground parking garage. We convinced the city that the residents ride bicycles instead and that they have sufficient parking spaces. We're currently navigating a regulation stipulating that rooftop solar panels must not be visible from street level. So we need to either hide them or install fewer panels. Much of our work involves discussing and negotiating ordinances with the city council. Although they understand that global warming must be addressed, the system gets in the way because it is so cumbersome.

Your office is at La Comunal, an industrial site that you converted into a cultural quarter. How is it now more climate-friendly?

EA We optimized its energy consumption. Building services and heated areas are reduced to a minimum, and most of the access areas are outside or only protected by a roof. Stairways between the buildings were outfitted with glass roofs – a feature we had to negotiate with the heritage preservation office. They serve as climate buffers, heating the air in winter and cooling it in summer, eliminating the need for air conditioners. We took a frugal approach to material procurement, repurposing slender old floor beams as roof shuttering, and sourcing insulation boards from a sandwich panel manufacturer to insulate the floor. Facades were reinforced by lime plaster mixed with cork. Under the courtyard, we installed a rainwater tank to collect water, which is used for watering plants. The plants are vital for cooling the courtyard, which will serve as a designated "climate shelter" where vulnerable groups can seek refuge if it becomes too hot at home. These climate shelters are required to maintain a temperature below 27 °C and be accessible within a five-minute timeframe. The city is expanding its climate shelter network, and our courtyard will be included once the plants have sufficiently grown.

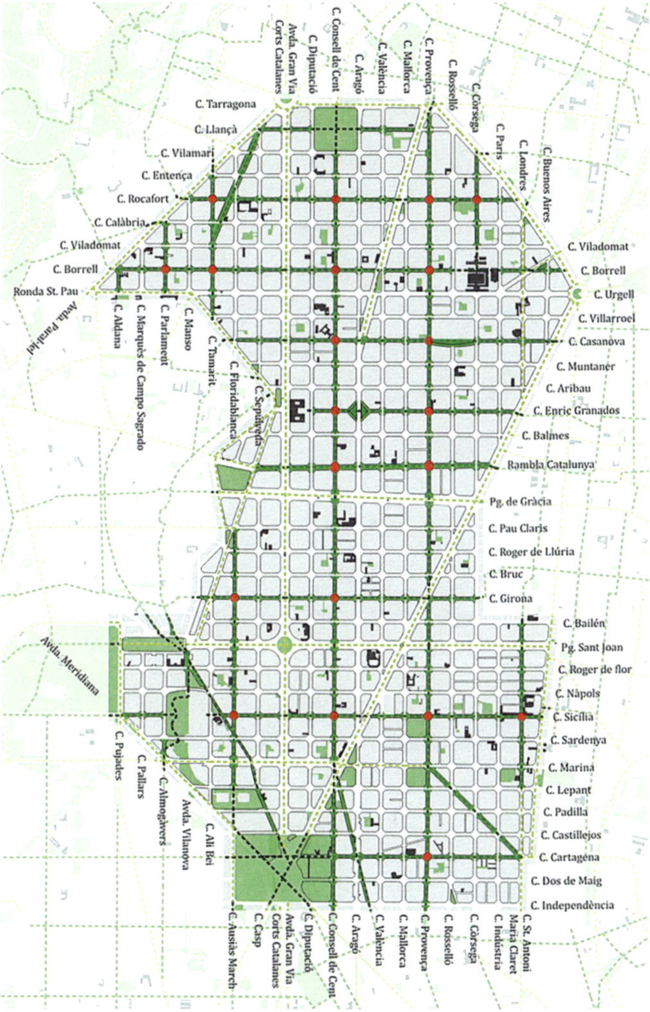

Barcelona is transforming into a city of "green axes" connecting traffic-calmed city blocks grouped into "superblocks".

Lacol

Design as a Problem Solver

Interview
Shigeru Ban

Shigeru Ban is both an architect and an activist. The Pritzker Prize laureate develops concepts for emergency shelters and prefers using renewable materials such as wood and paper. Jan Geipel spoke with Shigeru Ban in his office in the Tokyo district of Matsubara.

What are the most significant changes and challenges that have influenced your work since you were awarded the Pritzker Prize 10 years ago?

As you know, I have been working extensively in disaster areas. Until recently, mainly in areas which were hit by environmental disasters. Right now, I have an ongoing project in Ukraine. The tragedy is human-made and the poor shelter conditions are very similar to the ones we encounter after environmental disasters. I am collaborating with local architects and with the city of Lviv to build a hospital in timber. There are so many things architects can do here to improve the situation.

What motivated you to work on these challenges?

As an architect, I was disappointed with my own profession. We mainly work for privileged people. People who have power and money. But I started looking into social issues and began adapting my recycled paper constructions for use as disaster shelters. Before people started talking about ecology and sustainability, I was interested in using everyday materials, the materials that surround us, in an efficient way.

Circular thinking is deeply ingrained in Japanese culture. There is even a word for it, “mottainai”, a sort of no-waste philosophy. But nowadays, Japan seems to have turned into a throwaway-society. Almost any product here seems to be wrapped in multiple layers of single-use plastic. Why?

Shigeru Ban

I see your point, but I am likely not the right person to ask this question. I always reuse materials, for example paper. When I see my staff, I tell them to reuse things, to use both sides of sheets of paper, to deploy materials in an efficient way. All my handwritten notes and sketches are basically written and drawn on the reverse side of a sheet of waste paper. That should be the common way of dealing with things, also when choosing building materials.

Energy efficiency is now a major topic in the EU, especially the thermal insulation of buildings. How is the situation in Japan?

The regulations for energy, insulation, and environmental issues are becoming stricter here, too.

I recall your Curtain Wall House and especially the Naked House, both from the 1990s. Are these two buildings the conceptual opposite to European developments, something that would never be possible in the EU?

In Europe, you generally heat or cool all spaces, sometimes even 24 hours a day. The traditional Japanese way is different: We turn something on and then turn it off again. Take air conditioning, for example. We only switch it on in the rooms and areas we actually occupy. When we leave the space or leave the house, we switch it off or use a timer. We still use natural ventilation a lot. And we enjoy the interstitial spaces between inside and outside.

Do the tolerant regulations in Japan and the specific lifestyle of its people foster an architecture that is more innovative and flexible than in Europe?

The client desired a family home with an open design resembling a greenhouse. Shigeru Ban Architects completed the Naked House for them in 2000.

Paper Partition System 4, developed by Shigeru Ban in response to the 2011 earthquake in Japan, is a modular wall system using cardboard tubes and fabric providing privacy in emergency shelters.

In Japan, there are many opportunities for young architects to design private homes. The typology is great for both experimenting and training. Small house clients generally tend to be open-minded. Moreover, Japanese contractors actually support architects with their knowledge. As a result, we can make innovative houses with humble materials at a low cost. On the other hand, the quality of both public buildings and corporate headquarters in Europe is better than in Japan. In Japan, the CEOs often prefer hiring one of the big architecture firms to avoid risks, but the result is boring buildings.

In Europe, we generally build with very long timeframes in mind, several generations at least. In Japan, houses are usually torn down after 20 to 30 years. Why is that so?

There are several reasons for that. Earthquake regulations are becoming stricter, for example. So, often, we cannot preserve old buildings. And inheritance tax is very high. As a result, plots get divided in smaller units to share the costs, while the old houses are often demolished.

Would the Curtain Wall House or the Naked House still be possible in Japan today?

Yes, definitely! There aren't any strict regulations in place for private residential construction. The client of the Naked House asked for something very open and transparent, like a greenhouse. I am interested in creating architecture comparable to the human body: taking clothes off in summer, wearing more in winter – like insulation. I want to see buildings wearing different clothes. The skin of the building should be able to change.

At La Seine Musicale, the music and performing arts centre you designed near Paris, there is a big solar sail, circling on rails around the globe-shaped theatre, collecting energy, creating shade – and inspiring curiosity. Is using a form primarily in terms of its function a key approach to design on your part?

Precisely. Like Frei Otto, I am interested in "form finding" rather than "form making". I am not interested in the fashionable styles of the day. That is why I am still very fond of Frei Otto and Buckminster Fuller. Form has to be based on given requirements and has to take advantage of the context. If someone gives me a big site and a big budget, I start looking for problems that I can solve by design. So, my approach is rather "problem solving design".

"As an architect, I was disappointed with my own profession."

Shigeru Ban

Singapore as a Model Green City of the Future

Interview
Richard Hassell

Almost 6 million people live in Singapore on 730 km² – an area as large as Hamburg. In conversation with Barbara Zettel, Richard Hassell, co-founder of Woha architects, outlines his vision for Singapore in 2100 as a climate-positive megacity.

How is climate change affecting Singapore?

One of the gravest challenges is the sea level rise. The megacity has fully utilized its area and really has no hinterland. A rise of a few metres will cause it to lose nearly half of the land area, which is a problem for such a densely populated island. The Singapore government has been working on solutions for a couple of decades already. They have taken a defensive attitude, investing heavily in coastal protection and raising the ground level.

With "Singapore 2100", Woha has developed a vision for the island state in the 22nd century. How do you envision its future?

Singapore will be a liveable, sustainable, and resilient city of the 22nd century. It will be a city where humans and nature coexist in regenerative, circular systems. It will be even more lush and green and provide people with a great quality of life, with lots of amenities and community spaces that will encourage you to live a healthy and active lifestyle. It will have thriving biodiversity, be self-sufficient in renewable energy, water, and food, and carbon neutral in its operations and embodied energy.

Which strategies can help to achieve this?

Our idea is to reduce the urbanized coverage of Singapore to 50 %, to release land currently used for roads and other things back to nature. To do this, we need to think three-dimensionally, such as moving a lot of infrastructure underground and building upwards instead of continuing to push the city limits outwards. Singapore needs to grow vertically instead of horizontally. The city will be connected three-dimensionally: underground, on the surface, and in the air.

How realistic is this vision?

We think it's totally realistic. And it is probably easier to do in Singapore than in other places. Because it is a city-state and centrally planned, it's a lot easier to influence change than in many other places, which have separate federal, state, and local governments. Singapore is sometimes criticized for being very top-down in terms of policy. But with climate action, I think that is an advantage because it can react quickly to the gravity of the situation with appropriate measures.

What role does architecture play in this?

Speculative projects, like Singapore 2100, where we aim for big ideas and solve problems through design, form the backbone of our creative direction. With our architecture, we want to show how beautiful life in a regenerative world can be. With our projects, we are building prototypes for the city of the future. Our rating system uses five parameters to evaluate a building's performance: the green plot ratio, community plot ratio, civic generosity index, ecosystem contribution index, and the self-sufficiency index. Of course, we try to achieve high performance in all aspects, but in some projects, we focus more on maximizing greening, and in others, on communal use of the property. Each new project is like one piece of the puzzle of the future city.

Can you give us an example of such a prototype?

Kampung Admiralty is a public housing project for seniors and, like 80 % of Singapore's housing, was funded by the state

“If we could release 50% of the land back to nature in Singapore, it is possible to do it anywhere on the planet.”

Richard Hassell

Housing & Development Board (HDB). The project creates opportunities for intergenerational bonding and ensures that seniors are a part of a vibrant community. The lush greenery provides ecosystem services and a biophilic environment, and provides new habitats for biodiversity. There is even an urban farm at the top, where residents and neighbours can join a gardening club to plant and harvest fruits and vegetables.

What do you wish for the future?

I wish we could enter the regenerative phase and get over emissions so that cities are not a net-drain but net-positive for the planet. We should use our human ingenuity and ability to transform the Earth's surface and use it for good rather than destruction. I would really love for there to be a moratorium on all natural areas worldwide to prevent the destruction of nature and release areas back to nature, as suggested by Edward O. Wilson in his book "Half-Earth: Our Planet's Fight for Life". I would love for the United Nations to establish a policy that every state would commit to. It would be great if we could release 50 % of the land back to nature in the densely populated city-state of Singapore – that would show it's possible to do it anywhere on the planet.

Lush greenery on the terraced complex of Kampung Admiralty by Woha Architects provides residents with a natural environment and enhances the city's microclimate.

Richard Hassell

Corridors for Life

Interview
Richard Weller

With his vision of a World Park, American landscape architect Richard Weller proposes an interconnected network of biotopes that would stretch through 55 nations. Jakob Schoof spoke with him about it.

Your World Park is landscape design on the largest scale imaginable. What is the driving force behind your vision?

When you're a landscape architect dealing with the consequences of climate change, sooner or later, you think about big-picture issues. The designation of protected areas at the global level is usually not a matter for landscape or regional planning; the major environmental protection organizations and the United Nations handle that. As part of the UN Convention on Biological Diversity, 196 countries worldwide have committed to protecting a combined 17 % of their land area and 10 % of the world's oceans. And there are more and more designated protected areas around the world. But they are isolated from each other, like islands in an archipelago. Climate change is causing many species' habitats to change, and they need to migrate. That is not possible in a system of isolated protected areas. My vision of a networked World Park aims to connect habitats where biodiversity is exceptionally high.

How far along are we to achieving 17 % protected areas?

We are at 15.4 %. The difference doesn't sound that big, but it's still 700,000 times the area of Central Park in New York City. Some of the designated regions exist only on paper, or their protected status is unclear.

Would your World Park require humans to vacate the area entirely? Or could humans and nature coexist in the same space?

Richard Weller

The answer depends on your image of humanity. Traditional conservation, which emerged at the turn of the 20th century, held that humans should have no place in protected areas. As a result, Native Americans who had lived there for centuries were forced out of the United States national parks. Something similar happened in protected areas in Africa because the international conservation organizations based in Europe did not trust the local population. This led to a crisis of legitimacy – and a change in approach over the last 20 years. The World Park should not be a fenced reserve but an area where people live and work.

What kind of work?

New biodiversity corridors should be created between existing protected areas; much of that land has been used for monoculture farming. These corridors need to be planned, and the areas renaturalized; that also creates jobs.

That would mean buying the land from its previous owners – who is supposed to pay for that?

A lot of money has already been spent on developing protected areas. Much would be gained if these funds were redirected more towards the existing biodiversity hotspots connected by the World Park. Ultimately, the world's countries should pool their money, similar to the UN's Green Climate Fund, through which the world's wealthier nations plan to pay the poorer countries $100 billion every year for climate mitigation and adaptation. Financing the World Park would cost only a fraction of that amount.

What alliances have you formed to advance your vision?

I am in touch with stakeholders from science and business, the governments of the involved countries, and currently, with

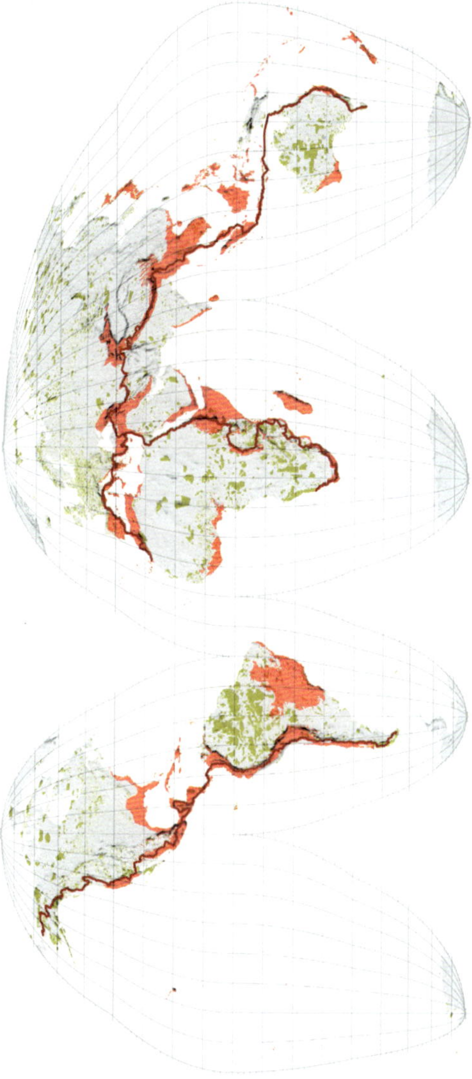

The World Park is envisioned as a global network of protected areas.

- Global Protected Areas
- Threatened Ecoregions
- World Park Trails

Richard Weller

Unesco. When I first presented my idea, even I had my doubts. I was afraid people would think I was a megalomaniac, or worse, that the World Park was a neocolonialist land grab. But nothing of the sort happened. The mainly positive response has motivated me to pursue the idea further.

How can architecture and landscape architecture foster biodiversity outside of protected areas?

Of course, it's not about having to share your home with wild animals in the future. Biodiversity already starts with ensuring more habitats for insects and less soil sealing. It also includes looking at the production of building materials and whether habitats are being destroyed in the process. In the past, when planning buildings and public spaces, the only users we considered were people. If we broaden our perspective to include other species, it opens up the horizon for design. And the result gives us a higher quality of life. Because living only among our own species all the time is like living in New York: it's exciting for a while, but at some point, it drives you crazy.

“If we broaden our perspective to other species, it opens up the horizon for design.”

Richard Weller

Circular and CO_2-neutral

Chapter 2

What to Do about the Climate Emergency?

Interview
Michael Pawlyn

Since 2019, over 6,000 offices in 20 countries have joined Architects Declare, a manifesto against climate change and for biodiversity. In an interview with Heide Wessely, Michael Pawlyn, British architect and co-initiator of Architects Declare, calls on colleagues to assume greater social responsibility for climate protection.

Tell us about Architects Declare; how did it start?

The October 2018 report from the Intergovernmental Panel on Climate Change (IPCC) gave us perhaps ten years to avoid catastrophic climate change and, at the time, there was a very limited level of response from the construction industry. In my own practice, I tried to implement exemplary sustainable projects with mixed success. I was always told that the market is not ready for these ideas yet. When I read the IPCC report I thought, "This is crazy! How can the market not be ready? We're this close to societal collapse." I reread one of my favourite essays by the American environmental scientist and systems thinker Donella Meadows, "Leverage Points: Places to Intervene in a System". It is not obvious where to act to bring about change in complex systems. She describes a list of 12 places to intervene in a system. I realized that I and many other architects had tried to act at too low a level. Right at the top is trying to change the paradigm, from which the system behaviour emerges. Steve Tompkins and I met in in a pub and discussed where each of us had agency – the capacity to influence things and bring about change. Steve's company had recently won the Stirling Prize, one of the highest UK prizes for architecture. We realized that he had some influence and imagined a joint declaration of as many Stirling Prize winners as possible, a declaration of climate and biodiversity emergency.

It's one thing for architects to agree, but how can Architects Declare convince the clients?

This is a broader issue within society. People tend to minimize their agency and architects often say, "There is not much we can do without a really good client"; people in the architectural press say, "We can only cover the stories which people want to read"; and even big client organizations say "We are answerable to our shareholders so there's not much we can do." A cycle of blame. The only way to change that is to maximize our agency. We are able to influence clients. Clients look to us to come up with ideas. An architect's role is not just to give the client what they say they want but also what they never thought possible.

How do Architects Declare members collaborate and share ideas?

Various ways. We invite speakers and we share knowledge in regular regional meetings and short presentations. We share successes and failures. The same happens on an international level. We have regular Zoom meetings with Architects Declare signatories from across the world – sometimes involving over 20 countries. We will soon issue a practice guide with practical advice on improving design performance, designing for zero operational carbon, zero embodied energy. And also, very importantly, how to shift from sustainable towards regenerative ways of designing.

How do countries with different cultural and economic backgrounds approach the topic?

Some are more active than others and some have cultural specificities – in Canada and Australia, indigenous knowledge and respecting indigenous people have become important. When Black Lives Matter became a major movement for change in the US, climate justice featured much more prominently in their declarations. And in the UK we're trying to catch up. For those unfamiliar with the term "climate justice", it refers to

“A cycle of blame. The only way to change that is to maximize our agency.”

Michael Pawlyn

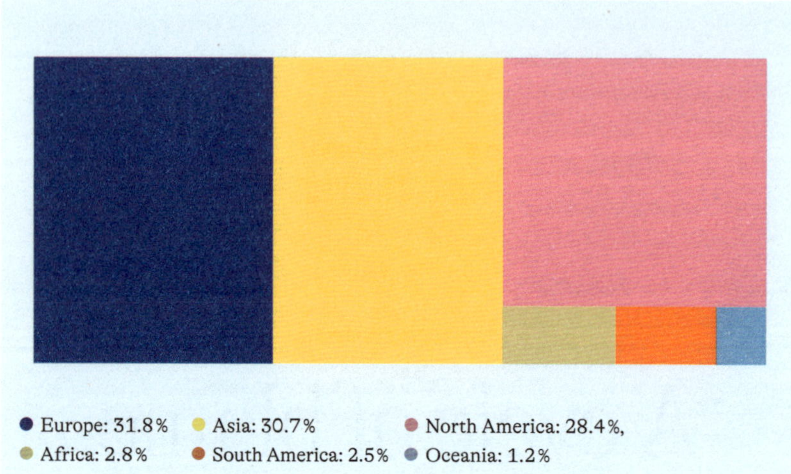

Breakdown by region of total CO_2 emissions accumulated by the year 2019 (figures in %; due to rounding, may not total 100% due to rounding).

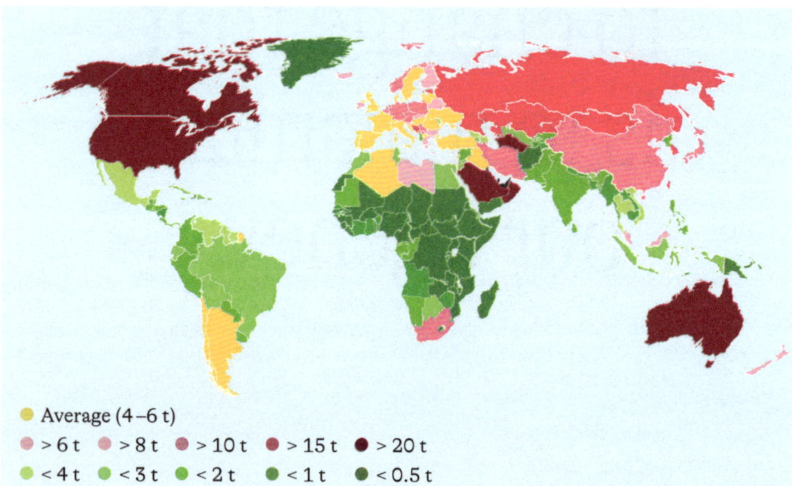

Annual CO_2 emissions per capita compared to the global average of 4.9 tonnes in 2019.

the intersection of climate change, racism, and global development efforts.. Developed nations have actually contributed by far the most to the problem of climate change and yet it's the poor countries that suffer the most. There is a strong argument that the developed countries should lead the way with the most stringent cuts to carbon emissions.

This won't be possible without political commitment; have you been met with support or ignorance or even hindrance?

This is a key part of our strategy for change, which evolved in a series of workshops with external consultants. The full aims of the declaration cannot be achieved at the level of an individual project or company, but only at a higher level. We are building the broadest possible coalition so that we can persuade governments. We have arranged meetings with the UK government, with mixed success, but we're not giving up. We stick to our guns and we will issue a set of policy demands for the UN Climate Change Conference in November 2021 (COP26), coordinated with the other Architects Declare countries. This represents the set of demands from over 6,000 companies around the world, and shows how we could rise to the challenge of climate change and biodiversity loss. If you, the UK government and other national governments, play your part, this is what we need you to do. That gives us a much more persuasive voice than if we just wrote to our members of parliament individually.

With the initiative "European Bauhaus", EU Commission President Ursula von der Leyen wants to unite sustainability and aesthetics in order to drive ecological change. Can this help us?

Not many details are available yet about the European Bauhaus, only that it sets out to be an ecological, economic, and cultural project to combine design, sustainability, accessibility, and investments. It is inclusive and establishes a connection with culture, which I like.

What we need is a societal shift, not just a shift in the technical design of buildings. We have thought hard about how change actually occurs. In the past, some changes seemed to be happening very slowly until a dramatic tipping point. For example, a friend of mine went to Berlin in 1989 and asked the family she stayed with, "Do you think the Wall will ever come down?" The father said, "No, that will never happen. Not in my lifetime." Three months later, it came down. And when she visited again half a year later, he told her, "Of course it was always going to happen." That was the tipping point where societal attitudes change profoundly. We need something similar in the construction industry. It's not enough to tighten up the bolts on the paradigm of sustainability. I hope that by joining up with lots of other Declare organizations and with public pressure we can help to bring about a tipping point and start to design in a way that could be continued indefinitely. Mitigating negative impact is not enough; we need net positive impact – not just as architects, but as industry, and in fact every realm of human activity. We need to get to the stage where everything we do has a net positive impact. A turning point in human civilization, and the sooner we get there, the better.

> There are signs that this might happen in the near future. The younger generation is fighting harder for their future than our generation ever was...

Absolutely. One point that I find interesting is that in most of the major social shifts that have happened in history, the last bastion of resistance is normally "angry old white men". The people criticizing Greta Thunberg are nearly all from that demographic. You could see that as a positive sign that we're close to a tipping point.

“What we need is a societal shift, not just a shift in the technical design of buildings.”

Michael Pawlyn

Radically Trans forming the Con struction Industry

Interview
Barbara Buser

With her practice Baubüro In Situ, Swiss architect Barbara Buser is committed to circular construction. She seeks simple solutions to reuse salvaged building components in her projects. A dialogue with Peter Popp.

The average temperature in Switzerland has increased by 2 °C compared to pre-industrial times – that's twice as much as the global average. What needs to change in the construction industry to stop climate change?

We need to radically transform the entire construction industry and make it circular. Right now, everything is linear. We take raw materials from nature, build something from them, and then – it's crazy – we tear them down 20 years later and throw the materials away. But if buildings are properly maintained, their lifespan in Switzerland could be hundreds of years. The much-discussed "sufficiency measures" imply that we need only to design processes more intelligently to save more resources. But that isn't enough because we live on a finite planet. If I had it my way, there would be a 10-year moratorium on new building materials. We should only be allowed to build with reused and renewable building materials and should rethink the entire supply and value chains.

Can you give us an example?

The concrete industry is making a great effort to work with recycled concrete. This will save us 3–5 % CO_2. With consistent reuse, we could save 80–90 %. For our renovation of a listed building at the Werkstadt complex in Zurich, we cut up concrete walls to use as foundation blocks. It's not always possible to do something like that, but it often is. You can make entire buildings from such blocks.

Barbara Buser

The K.118 pilot project at the Sulzer complex in Winterthur was supposed to be built using 100 % recycled components. Did you reach your target?

Technically, 100 % would have been possible. But due to financial issues, we reached 70 %. We also ran up against psychological limits. Some companies simply have no interest in making parts less expensive or keeping things running longer; they want to sell new building parts.

The K.118 project description states that circular building means "thinking in loops". What exactly does that mean?

With each component you find, you have to revise your design. The entire planning process essentially goes in a circle. It begins with the search for materials, adapting to the situation and available materials. We were fortunate enough to secure a steel structure at one of our other sites. The new supporting structure on top of Hall 118 once supported an old distribution centre at the Lysbüchel complex in Basel, which we were converting into the Elys cultural and commercial centre around the same time. Searching for available components is quite fast nowadays and does not pose any problems. You just have to be more modest about what is possible and obtainable instead of mindlessly ordering from the building industry's global product catalogue.

Does reuse also mean abandoning predefined aesthetic ideals?

I don't think so. But you have to give up the idea of free choice. For the Elys project, we used green trapezoidal sheeting from the previous roof installations to achieve a uniform facade design. We also calculated whether they would be worth reusing if their surfaces were freshly painted. New panels cost

Built mainly from salvaged construction materials in 2021, the extension by Baubüro In Situ crowns Hall 118 (K.118) at the Sulzer complex in Winterthur. The hall now houses 12 studios, creative spaces, and a tinkering lab on the ground floor.

Barbara Buser

45 CHF per square metre. Fetching them from the demolition site, transporting them on pallets, cleaning them, and reusing them costs 10 CHF less per panel. However, after repainting, they would cost 90 CHF. So that made no sense at all. Ultimately, you have to consider your sense of aesthetics: Do you like patina or not?

Are used materials otherwise financially worthwhile?

For K.118, we asked the clients to give us CHF 500,000 in advance – about 10 % of the total construction costs. That allowed us to search for, disassemble, inspect, and temporarily store the salvaged materials. The amount was almost enough. This means 10 % of the total construction costs were invested in salvaged materials. New components cost about the same. So recycling must not and will not cost more than new material in the future. Ideally, it should be even cheaper.

How about the effort?

That is still relatively large at the moment. We employed four people as material hunters. They bike through the city, scan newspaper demolition ads, painstakingly research who is responsible, and lead us to the resources. On the other hand, I get phone calls daily from people telling me they have three windows left on their work site because of wrong deliveries. The process is disheartening: this isn't how planning should be. We cannot be like scavengers who use what nobody else wants and sometimes even have to pay to pick it up.

What do you propose as a solution?

25 years ago, I founded Bauteilbörse Basel (Basel building parts exchange) and developed a database to offer used components online. It still exists today and is now called Use Again. The problem is that a lot of individual components are

"We cannot be like scavengers who use what nobody else wants."

Barbara Buser

Old lockers now serve as safety barriers in the new K.118 workshop area.

still advertised there. But we need to get to an industrial scale, otherwise, the impact is just too low. To do so, we need to work with the demolition companies, especially the planners and owners. Large property owners need to advertise now what they plan to demolish in the next few years. The best would be if they could manage circularity within their own buildings, which would solve all the warranty issues. Circular construction processes can only be planned well if everyone takes part.

How creative do you have to be to transfer materials to other contexts of use?

With K.118, we reused double-glazed industrial windows. Alone, they no longer met the regulations, so we simply doubled them up to build box windows, which more than met the regulations. There is so much available!

Are there any legal hurdles to reusing building materials?

The window issue – my favourite topic – is exemplary. You can upgrade virtually any window so it meets the standards. 600 windows with double insulated glass can be converted to 400 with triple insulated glass. It's sensible and not more expensive than new windowpanes. It may not be perfect, but it serves the purpose. A lot is possible, and we work open source. To save time, we have shared all our experiences in the book "Bauteile wiederverwenden" (Reusing Building Materials).

What do you tell architects who claim they can reuse their new building at the end of its life cycle?

Sorry, that's too late. What shall we do in 60 years? If we continue like this, we won't get very far. The basic idea is correct, but it should have been adopted 50 years ago. At the moment, it's no use at all.

What gives you hope nonetheless?

I spent three weeks dismantling building materials on construction sites with my students at ETH Zurich. They used that to build a pavilion in two months with their own hands. That was impressive. Their inventiveness and ingenuity give me a bit of hope that maybe we'll make it after all.

2,000 m² of old corrugated aluminium were dismantled on site and repurposed for the facade of the Elys cultural and commercial building at the Lysbüchel complex in Basel.

Barbara Buser

Who Will Run the Urban Mines of the Future?

Interview
Anders Lendager

Danish architect Anders Lendager is one of the most radical pioneers of circular construction. In this interview with Jakob Schoof, he explains how architects can help end the throwaway society.

You are an architect, but you also run a consulting firm and, until recently, have been involved in a number of companies that manufacture building products. How did that come about?

As an architect, I know that clients ask about cost whenever the subject of sustainability comes up and I've seen how little established manufacturers cared about recycling building materials. So I realized that I had to take care of those things myself. Today, we advise companies and municipalities who want to find out what materials are used in their building stock. This often leads to building projects for my architectural practice – and in turn to a demand for upcycled building products. To satisfy it, until a few weeks ago I ran a development and production company for recycled building products. I have now sold this company to investors, which I think is a milestone for the circular business model that we have established.

That's not an everyday business model for an architect.

In my case, it was necessary. And I think as architects we can't afford in the long run to always be drawing grand plans and letting others bear the financial risk for them.

What kind of clients do you mainly work with? Private, public, commercial?

All of them. Five years ago it was very different: back then, when you talked to representatives of the big Danish pension funds, they were happy to listen to your ideas – and as soon as you left, they were done with the subject. Nowadays we work with the most conservative investors you can imagine – and they see that they can make money with circular construction. But it should all go much faster. Consumers are often smarter than the industry; they want to live sustainably, and the demand for ecological solutions is so great that the construction industry can't keep up with deliveries.

> You also advise local authorities and companies who want to know what materials are used in their building stock. To what end?

Previously, when these companies wanted to demolish a building and rebuild on the property, they paid the demolition contractor a flat rate. With our method, they can now find out exactly how much concrete, glass, and steel are in a building, what these materials are worth, and how they can be recycled or reused. This gave them a much better bargaining chip on demolition costs. We also show how much money they can save by reusing these materials in new construction. This is where things get really interesting for many investors.

> Building materials in existing stock are often contaminated with invisible pollutants like asbestos or PCBs. How problematic is that?

There are now sophisticated methods for measuring the pollutant load of building materials even before demolition. Even if it turns out that 3 % of the building contains pollutants, you can still reuse 97 % of the materials. Here in Denmark we examined buildings from the 1970s whose precast concrete elements are contaminated with PCBs. When heated, the PCB volatilizes. So we built a kind of large oven out of a container in which we thermally decontaminated the concrete elements.

Upcycle Studios is a townhouse development in Copenhagen by Lendager Architects utilizing construction materials repurposed from other projects.

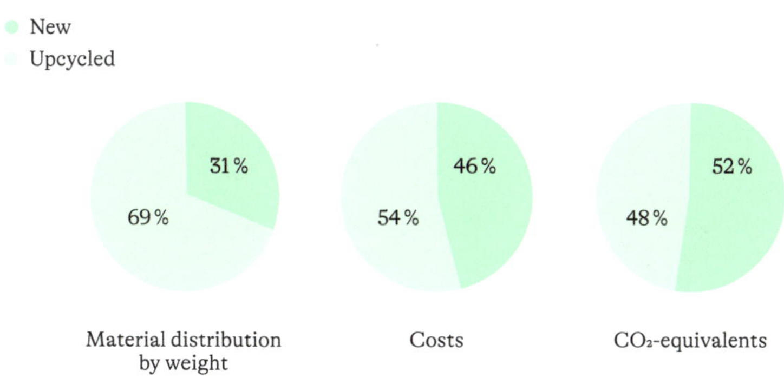

Anders Lendager

Resource Rows, a residential complex in the Ørestad neighbourhood of Copenhagen by Lendager Architects, features a patchwork facade of upcycled brick panels.

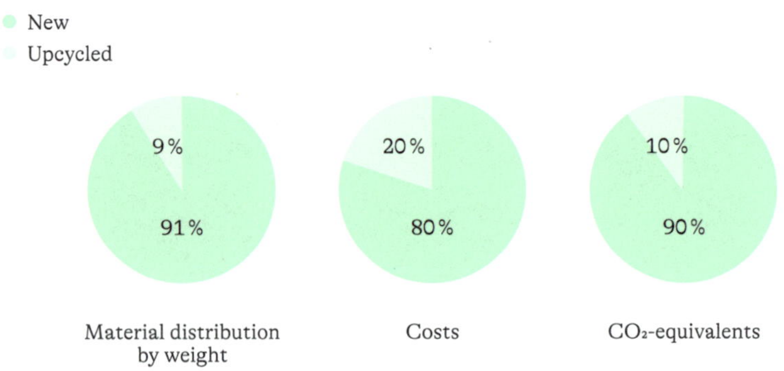

You say that recycled building materials don't have to cost more, and are often cheaper than new ones. What can be done to ensure this actually happens?

Of course, it depends on what you're reusing. For example, decking from reclaimed wood is easier to produce at a competitive cost than recycled concrete or the brick facades for our Resource Rows project in Copenhagen. But as a rule, the building products we develop from recycled material aren't more than 10 % more expensive than new comparable products. And after we use them on two or three construction projects and increased their production volume accordingly, they often become 50 to 70 % cheaper.

In Europe, you need approval for reused materials. Doesn't that complicate the process?

Not more than if you build with new materials. The load-bearing capacity of old steel or concrete beams can be tested and fire protection tests can be carried out with reused materials. I'm probably the best known architect to the Danish fire authorities because I'm always showing up with the craziest materials to get tested! The warranty isn't a big drama either. A good window lasts for 50 years. So if we remove an existing window after 10 or 15 years and install it in a new house, we can also give a five-year guarantee on it. Where's the problem?

To what extent does the availability of materials influence your design aesthetic?

That's an important question I often address: Should recycled materials in buildings be recognizable as such? We have already used both strategies in our projects. If the materials are left visible, they can tell their story. The residents at Resource Rows in Copenhagen, for example, know exactly where the bricks for their building come from. This allows them to develop a much closer relationship with their home than they would in a new build. But it doesn't always work that way. With recycled glass panes or recycled concrete, for example, it's not apparent that they were previously used. That raises another point: if you reuse windows in a building, the facade design must be based on their dimensions and proportions. That's why the City of Copenhagen granted us building permits for some of our projects without knowing exactly what the whole thing would look like in the end. Of course, this also requires courage on the part of the administration.

What needs to happen for your way of thinking and working to become commonplace in the construction industry?

The impulse might come from a very unexpected direction. A few years ago, no one thought I would get into concrete recycling. But to advance the idea of circular construction, we must influence the materials that are used in our buildings. Mies van der Rohe knew exactly which marble he wanted to use in the Barcelona Pavilion. Today, many architects choose the colours for their buildings at best. This is where we need to regain control: we should be builders again, not surface designers. That doesn't mean we have to get into building materials production ourselves. But we can forge alliances with companies. These won't always be the major construction suppliers; smaller firms are often much better positioned.

“We should be builders again, not surface designers.”

Anders Lendager

What needs to change at the political level?

I have spent a lot of time advising ministries and other agencies. Unfortunately, it's hard to make progress because here in Denmark the government changes every few years and then you have to start over from scratch. We can no longer wait for politics, but must become active ourselves. Ultimately, I also realized my projects under the prevailing conditions. And you know that when you point your fingers at others, at least three fingers point back at you.

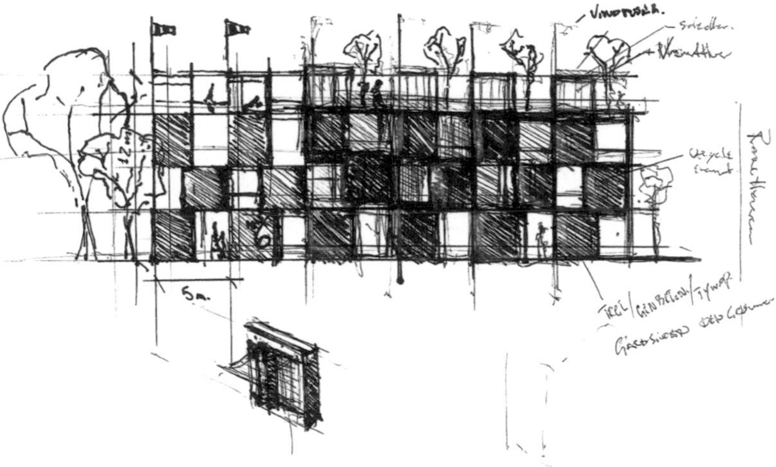

The facade design is based on the dimensions and proportions of the recycled components.

How Do We Shift to Sustain able Construc tion?

Interview
Lamia Messari-Becker

Lamia Messari-Becker is a leading voice on sustainable construction. The professor at the University of Siegen serves as a policy advisor on various committees. In an interview with Julia Liese, she discussed her ideas for how the construction sector can address climate change.

What changes are needed to make the construction industry more sustainable?

The short answer: We need to change how we manage all our resources, including space, building materials, raw materials, energy, and, of course, money. Achieving this not only requires strong support for innovation and research but above all comprehensive policy changes.

What about the circular economy and policies for reusing building materials?

Using resource passports that track a building's material usage and carbon emissions makes sense to me. I don't think we should impose strict limits right away. Instead, we should encourage and nurture the innovative ideas already present in the construction sector. For instance, some buildings generate surplus energy throughout their lifecycle, while others are fully recyclable or climate neutral. I could also imagine introducing a permit for dismantling that would require anyone constructing a new building to outline how it could eventually be reused or redeveloped sustainably.

How can we increase the repurposing and conversion of existing buildings instead of the common practice of demolishing and replacing them?

We need to overhaul construction regulations and enact laws specifically focused on building renovation. Currently, the challenges already begin with the designated use defined in the development plan. The legislation needs to be more flexible so that you can turn a hotel into a dormitory or a housing complex into a school. Moreover, we need to reform technical standards so that conversions have less stringent requirements. Currently, conversions must meet the same specifications as new buildings for thermal insulation, soundproofing, and fire protection. But it should be simpler to adapt and repurpose existing structures. We currently have over 3,800 building regulations and directives. Our outdated building code and its cumbersome bureaucracy have been around for over 50 years. It's urgent that we envision a more forward-focused code.

Space utilization is another major challenge in Germany, especially with the need to construct 400,000 new apartments. How do we resolve this challenge?

My guiding principle is: improve the inside before the outside. Adding extra levels and extensions can create more living space without significantly expanding a building's footprint. For instance, at the Platensiedlung estate in Frankfurt am Main, over 670 additional apartments were created simply by adding new stories and a couple of end buildings. Once the potential for densification is exhausted, we can turn to new construction. But merely building on greenfield sites without sufficient infrastructure will mean that people will have to drive into the city to work or shop. In other words, it shifts emissions and resource consumption from the building to the streets. Likewise, if buildings are designed solely to improve heating efficiency, adding materials and technology to meet strict energy standards merely transfers emissions from the operational phase to the construction phase. A more balanced approach is essential.

Concrete's grey energy impact is concerning. How about building only with clay, wood, and straw?

“Our outdated building code and its cumbersome bureaucracy have been around for over 50 years. It is urgent that we envision a more forward-focused code.”

Lamia Messari-Becker

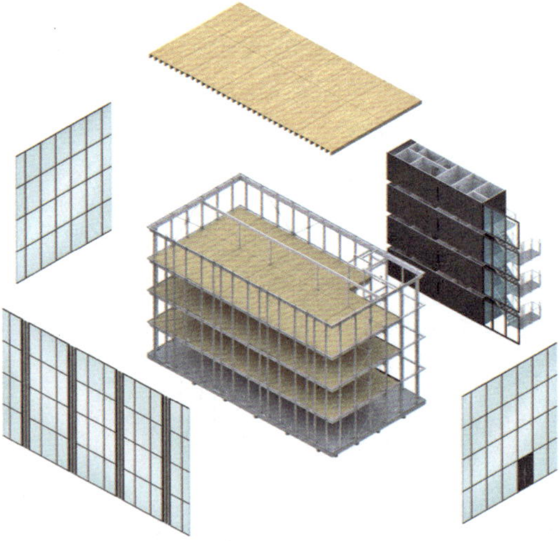

Circular economy: The Building D(emountable) office building in Delft by Cepezed is designed to be dismantled into individual parts for reuse.

Wood is an excellent building material with a positive ecological footprint and good insulation properties. However, timber buildings may require cooling in summer, which is four times more energy-intensive than heating. We must adopt a nuanced perspective toward building materials. Concrete has drawbacks, like its CO_2-intensive production with cement, but it also offers benefits, such as its high loadbearing capacity, resilience, and durability. I believe we need all materials: concrete, steel, wood, clay, masonry, brick, glass, plastic. Having this diversity is a strength that enables us to select the right material combinations for each task. There is a clear need to improve the sustainability of these materials. With concrete, for instance, I expect better recyclability and material efficiency, and with timber, more sustainable forestry. But the discussion must go beyond building materials to include forward-thinking construction methods that are both reversible and adaptable.

> Whether a building is made of concrete or wood is ultimately decided by the client. How can architects actively contribute to a better climate?

Planners wield significant influence through their recommendations. In my experience, there are always clients willing to explore new avenues and invest in sustainable solutions. But public sector procurement should also prioritize sustainability criteria. Choosing the lowest bid can become expensive in the long run. It is smarter to consider costs over a project's entire lifecycle. Who better than the public sector should lead in this regard?

> Are there any countries that stand out as role models for sustainable construction?

No country gets everything perfect in construction, but we can learn from each other in specific areas. The Dutch excel in space efficiency, Sweden leads with its carbon tax, Switzerland excels in recycling, and Denmark pioneered neighbourhood-focused approaches.

Can you explain that further?

By considering not just individual buildings but whole urban quarters during planning, we can unlock numerous synergies – from collective renovation initiatives to mobility plans and energy supply strategies. This is why I also advocate shifting funding policies away from individual projects and towards neighbourhood-based programmes. A holistic approach is crucial, and would accelerate our progress toward climate protection goals.

As an expert and advisor, you participate in various political committees. What topics are discussed there?

Topics include environmental protection, biodiversity, transportation, infrastructure, digitalization, energy, and climate protection – as well as construction and urban development. Some panels produce short, concise recommendation papers, while others spend several years producing in-depth studies. Ultimately, it's about providing advice and recommendations. In the end, the decisions rest in the hands of the politicians.

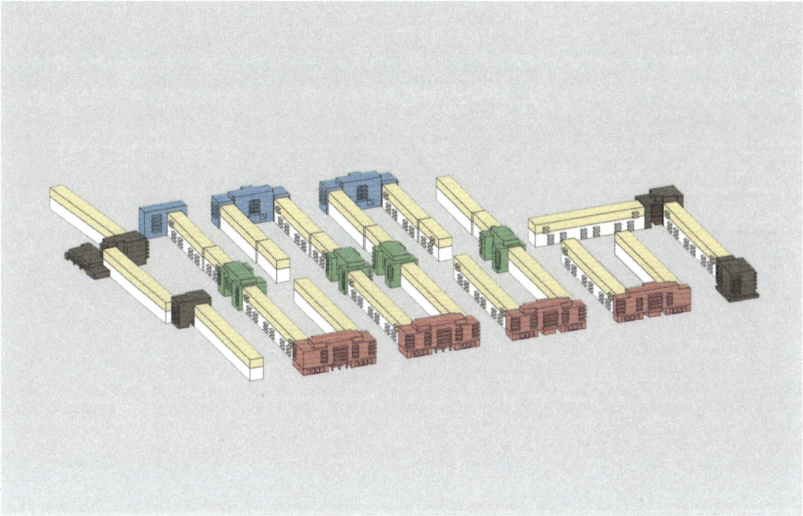

Urban densification: At the Platensiedlung housing development in Frankfurt, Stefan Forster Architekten added extra floors and extensions to the xisting buildings, creating 688 new apartments.

Lamia Messari-Becker

Building in Material Cycles

Interview
Catherine De Wolf

Catherine De Wolf conducts research and teaches about the circular economy at the ETH Zurich. With the help of digital tools, she connects recycled building materials, potential users, and projects. A conversation with Frank Kaltenbach.

You have been working on material cycles in the construction industry for over a decade, but the topic has only recently become a major talking point. How do you feel about it going from a niche issue to a general trend?

It was long overdue that we stop defining sustainability solely in terms of the energy needed to operate a building. Most of the award-winning, energy-saving buildings require immense amounts of grey energy. So their life cycle balance for energy consumption usually isn't as golden as their medal for energy consumption. High energy standards often lead to the unnecessary demolition of older buildings because retrofitting seems too costly from a technical and economic perspective. Buildings pegged for demolition are already being inspected for recyclable materials – there's much money to make from them. The circular economy is often confused with downcycling high-value building materials for use as fill material in road construction. Today, everyone is talking about cradle-to-cradle, but far less than 1 % of materials are reused in construction. Its mostly aluminium or glass, which are newly mined in Europe only to a minimal extent.

Why is the material cycle in construction still in its infancy?

We are currently analysing just that. Besides technical and legal hurdles, there is a huge information and communication deficit. That's where we want to start, using digital tools to connect people, projects, and products as efficiently as possible.

What will this digital networking work look like?

In other industries, digital platforms were quickly established to link service providers and potential users worldwide. If we want to connect the entire society in a circular economy, we need something like an Uber or Airbnb for the construction industry so that people interested in recycled building materials can find suitable demolition projects in their area.

Will every building cleared for demolition and all its materials be listed in a public database?

We could go even further and create a digital record of the materials used for new buildings for future reuse.

Wouldn't a comprehensive component database be too much work?

Much data is freely available; it only needs to be appropriately evaluated and processed. As a faculty member at the ETH AI Center for artificial intelligence, I am networked with AI research institutions across Europe. With the right algorithms, AI can search Google Street View footage for vacant lots and empty buildings. Entering the results into GIS – the government geographic information system that covers all of Switzerland – yields a digital map for potential urban mining. If property owners could also be viewed transparently, interested parties could contact them directly. Blockchain technology, i.e., decentralized data management systems, could optimize processes even further.

ETH has done pioneering work with construction robots. Can you tap this deep experience for your work?

Our Circular Engineering for Architecture Lab is part of the Digital Fabrication Lab (dfab) at the National Center of Competence in Research (NCCR), where we collaborate with the

“If we want to connect the entire society in a circular economy, we need something like an Uber or Airbnb for the construction industry.”

Catherine De Wolf

Robotics Systems Lab and the Gramazio Kohler Research Group. Construction robots or drones can photograph each component and mark it with a QR code, and laser scanners help us analyse the demolition materials.

How do your recycled pavilions work?

On a small scale, robots can already help dismantle a building into its parts and sort them. Our material resource was an old music pavilion. We carefully disassembled it and separated the materials as part of a student project. After sorting, each component was marked with a QR code and its data – such as material, cross-section, and length – was entered into the database. We then used this data to design a pavilion dome built entirely from demolition materials with almost no offcuts. In June 2023, we will build another pavilion from the dismantled Huber Pavilions at ETH from the 1930s. As researchers, we don't want to write long scientific papers that get attention in academia at best, but rather explore specific areas of action that can be scaled up for the construction industry and implemented on a large scale in the construction process. Our design-build projects are not just hands-on exercises for students but also intended to provide new insights for science.

To what extent is the circular construction scene networked with each other?

In Switzerland, there is the Circular Hub, an internet platform that issues publications on that topic; as well as Cirkla, an umbrella organization for reuse in the construction industry. Cross-border cooperation still needs to be intensified in order to facilitate short-distance material transports to neighbouring countries, as in the border region around Basel.

Where has this networking been successful?

Materials salvaged from an old music pavilion were used to construct a new pavilion on the ETH Zurich campus in 2022. The new pavilion was built using the old beams, with next to zero waste.

Catherine De Wolf

Demolition materials are sorted by hand and with the help of laser scanners and robots, then marked with QR codes and recorded in a database.

There are pioneers in Switzerland, such as Baubüro in situ with their circular projects. However, many collaborations still come about by chance or through personal contacts. During the renovation of the Centre Pompidou 2020, the architecture team at the planning firm Elioth wrote a book on how to reuse the building's old glass, but they didn't find a suitable project for it. At that time, I was a visiting researcher at Elioth. I launched a call for projects through my network and got in touch with Maximum architecture. They could reuse 178 curved windows from the escalator tubes to construct for small workrooms in the hall of an administrative building. The disassembly required suction lifters and was technically challenging and time-consuming. Still, the new owner of the glass paid less than what it would have cost new. If such classics of architectural history were listed in databases as urban mining resources, interested parties would undoubtedly be easier to find. With iconic buildings like Centre Pompidou or Mies van der Rohe's New National Gallery, there would certainly be modernism lovers for whom price would not be a primary consideration.

Catherine De Wolf

Building without Waste

Interview
Michael Braungart

If we want to have a waste-free circular economy, the business models in the construction industry need to change, explains Michael Braungart, inventor of the cradle-to-cradle principle in a conversation with Jakob Schoof and Barbara Zettel.

Mr. Braungart, you founded the Environmental Protection Encouragement Agency (EPEA) in 1987. Soon after, you began advising firms whose factories you and Greenpeace had once protested against. What prompted this change?

I had been protesting with Greenpeace for years, jamming factory pipes, riding rubber dinghies, occupying smokestacks, and swimming through the North Sea in order to stop ships. At some point I told myself: Now is the time to develop solutions. After all, I'm a chemist and a process engineer. The original purpose of EPEA was to offer scientific background data for the work conducted by environmental organisations. We trained activists for Greenpeace all over the world. And we developed solutions, for instance, a process that allowed bleaching cellulose without chlorine. Another project was the first CFC-free refrigerator, which I developed together with five other scientists.

In the meantime, many corporations are setting ambitious climate targets and are legally obligated to publish sustainability reports. Is this a step forward?

Sustainability consultants and rapporteurs are my greatest enemies! The consulting industry makes tons of money by releasing environmental reports. Corporate sustainability officers are often no more than the appendix of a PR division. The only thing they do is report on things. Maybe two more electric cars are connected to the grid. Or someone opens an insect hotel. Or prints the sustainability report on recycled paper and increases the recycling quota of plastic bottles by 2 %. That isn't what real change looks like.

Michael Braungart

You repeatedly deliver harsh critique of the concept of sustainability. Why?

Because it is a tragic concept. Just think about the original motivation behind the 1987 Brundtland Report: To meet the needs of today's generation without harming tomorrow's generations. Now just imagine this: You come home from work and you tell your kids: "I won't harm you today." That doesn't make any sense! We need concepts with a positive outlook, instead of debates focused on abstinence. Typically, people are generous and kind. Unless they have the feeling that somebody wants to take something away from them.

In your book "Cradle to Cradle", you evoke the image of a blooming cherry tree in order to explain why wastefulness is not bad as such. But is it really sensible for us to practice wastefulness in todays' world?

We could call it a culture of being generous. Nature, with its materials, forms, and colours, exemplifies this. To do the same also means that we need to employ proper energy sources. As long as that isn't the case, we have to reduce, avoid, conserve. However, I believe that the problem with energy can be solved. The problem with materials is a much more critical one.

How can we apply your notion of being generous to the construction field?

We should use our design freedom to create space for other living beings. For instance, if we add habitats for sparrow hawks or bats to single family homes, we can forget the debates about outlawing them.

What about the impact of sprawl on landscapes and the mobility requirements that result from single-family homes?

"Nature displays wastefulness in terms of materials, forms, and colours. To do the same means we need to use proper energy sources."

Michael Braungart

The Triodos Bank office building in Driebergen-Rijsenburg, designed by Rau Architecten, features a demountable wood-hybrid structure. All materials are recyclable and documented in a materials passport.

We already inhabit a cultural landscape. Old-growth forests no longer really exist in central Europe. Why don't we conceive landscapes as gardens, including the buildings situated within them? For instance, by using facades for the production of algae, we can create as much protein on one hectare of facade surface as on 60 ha of cornfields. That already saves us a significant amount of food transports.

> Particularly in that field, the demand for cradle-to-cradle (C2C) certifications has strongly increased. Who is driving this demand?

At the moment, Drees & Sommer is certainly a significant driver. The firm merged with EPEA in 2019. One precondition for the merger was that they apply C2C principles to all of their upcoming projects. This actually works. However, many manufacturers add surcharges to the costs for C2C products. Neither architects nor their clients should tolerate this! On average, these products are 20 % less expensive across their entire lifecycle compared to conventional products – because they were planned in an intelligent manner from the start. As a result, you can forget filters, occupational safety and health measures, or warehousing. The problem is that companies want to see returns on their development costs for these products within the shortest possible amount of time. The costs for one of our projects in Essen increased by 800,000 euros due to such eco-surcharges.

> What needs to change in order to reduce costs for C2C products?

Firstly, the business models! Novo-Tech, a company from Aschersleben, produces terrace decking made of so-called wood plastic composites. They substitute any and all tropical wood species. However, their customers only purchase the right-of-use, which means that the building becomes a materials bank. The material can be reused up to 30 times for the same purpose. As a result, the company owns sufficient raw materials for the next 900 years of business. If I were a manufacturer and would no longer sell floorboards or carpet flooring, but instead, only the right-of-use, I would employ the best possible material. I would no longer have to compromise between costs and quality. Solar power systems are another example: The manufacturer needs to maintain ownership over the product. The German manufacturers had actually offered modules that maintained 92 % of their efficiency following 20 years of operation. The modules produced by the Chinese competition lost half of their efficiency within the first five years. But they were 30 % less expensive. If German manufacturers had leased their modules instead of selling them, they would now be the global market leaders.

The concept of C2C is anticipatory: Let us build today by establishing closed material cycles for the future. What can we do about existing buildings built according to everything else except C2C principles?

I remain sceptical when it comes to renovations with amortization periods spanning 30 years and more. Let's say I have 100,000 euros to spend. There are hundreds of more effective ways of using this money instead of adding insulation to a building. Not only do we stick layers of styrofoam to building facades, we also try to make them airtight! The indoor air quality of buildings is three to eight times worse than the outdoor air in cities. We should ask: How can we achieve healthy air quality? Instead of: How can we create an airtight building envelope?

Reports state that more than 80 % of construction waste in Germany is recycled – but only as infill for earthworks and for roadbeds. This is particularly the

Wulf Architekten designed a fire station in Straubenhardt with a timber structure and expanded metal facade rising from a concrete base. The wooden elements are bolted together without any adhesives, paint, or plaster.

Michael Braungart

Kada Wittfeld Architektur designed the RAG Zollverein new headquarters in Essen to innovative sustainability standards based on the Cradle to Cradle approach. The building received the highest DGNB Certificate in Platinum.

case for mineral-based construction materials. Should we use them less?

Look at the components! Take concrete, where more than one hundred admixtures come into play – release agents, plasticizers, stabilizers. Recycled concrete is actually a different kind of hazardous waste. Gypsum is another problem: the amount of recycled gypsum produced by flue gas desulphurization is decreasing, because coal power plants are being decommissioned. This will increase the demand for gypsum from natural deposits. In general, mineral based construction materials are fine. Take the Cologne Cathedral: it's mineral-based and built to last forever. All additions and expansions need to be designed in a way that allows repeatedly reusing the selected materials.

What about timber construction?

Timber construction won't save us – at least not in its current form. The decisive aspect is how we treat timber. Ten years ago I offered my advice to a producer of construction paint. None of their wood paint products allowed risk-free composting or burning without use of complex filter systems. Today, dozens of wood paint products are available that pose no such risks.

Certain components are difficult to recycle, yet often the cheapest. How to deal with this?

We have to take the market economy seriously. At the moment, some reap the rewards while others are exposed to the risks. This is unacceptable. If manufacturers retain the responsibility for a product throughout the entire lifecycle, they will soon develop better solutions. The reason is that they will otherwise have to deal with the resulting waste – and not only benefit from their profit.

Michael Braungart

Should we reduce the diversity of construction materials altogether?

Recently we identified 52 different types of plastic in use for a discounter's store brand items alone. That is nonsense, there is no way to recycle that.

How do you envision the future?

Let's take people seriously! They want to do good, given the opportunity. And we need a positive outlook for that. For instance: By 2100, let's reduce CO_2 in the atmosphere to the level of the year 1900. Or, let's develop types of plastic that can be endlessly reused in buildings. If we only increase the recyclable portion by 3% for problematic materials such as PVC, nobody will care.

“Let’s take people seriously! They want to do good, given the opportunity.”

Michael Braungart

Resources and Reserves

Chapter 3

A Dance between Old and New

Interview
Inge Vinck

With modest budgets and well-considered concepts, architecten Jan De Vylder Inge Vinck (AJDVIV) in Ghent adapts existing structures for flexible future uses. In our interview, Inge Vinck discusses her approach to adaptive reuse with Sandra Hofmeister.

Many of your projects involve adapting existing structures. What is your strategy for dealing with this challenging design task?

As architects, it is our duty to engage with built environments. Today, so much has been built already, and there are limited plots available for new buildings. We should also be conscious of preserving the few natural spaces we still have. Our approach to dealing with existing contexts varies from project to project, depending on the client, available budget, and regulations. We start with what is given, which includes not only the building itself but also many other considerations. From there, we try to introduce the required programme.

Does this mean you are generally confident that all existing buildings have a future?

For us, it is important to address existing structures in a way that makes them adaptable for different uses in the future, long after our intervention. We prepare buildings for the future, providing an immediate purpose with the client while accounting for other possible functions over time. In this way, we ensure that buildings can thrive, protecting them from decay and offering a forward-looking perspective.

How do you manage needs and functions when adapting existing structures?

House Rot-Ellen-Berg near Ghent used to be a cafe before we renovated it in 2013. The building was too large for the family that wanted to use it as a new home, so we removed the floors and ceilings. Then we essentially built a new house within the old one, using the typical props and tables you often find on construction sites to create floors and walls. These systems are usually temporary, but we transformed them into permanent building components. This approach reduced costs and made the construction straightforward. It was also an ideal solution for our clients, who wanted to build their house themselves because of their limited budget. The installations can be removed easily through a do-it-yourself approach, making the old structure available again for something else – for a new future.

> You also took an unconventional approach when adapting the Caritas building.

We decided to create a square-like atmosphere within the existing volume, with community areas on different levels. It felt like everything we needed was already there: the building itself and the spaces within it – It was just a matter of looking at the existing structures differently and reinventing how to inhabit them. By removing some elements, the building became an open space while retaining its original volume. This enables it to be used in different ways and accommodate new programmes in the future.

> This approach likely requires bold investors and clients, doesn't it?

Many investors assume that old buildings cannot be adapted to new uses. However, we believe it is always possible to find ways to do this and make existing buildings compliant with new regulations. The more you engage with existing structures and navigate the regulations, the more clear it becomes that cost-effective adaptations are achievable. As architects, we have the huge task of changing investors' perspectives,

Manifesto for adaptive reuse: For the Caritas building in Melle, Belgium, Jan de Vylder, Inge Vinck und Jo Taillieu combined new concrete blocks with the historic brickwork.

Inge Vinck

encouraging them to look beyond maximizing square metres. It is in their interest to focus more on creating interesting, quality spaces.

> Can you describe the relationship between old and new in your projects?

We see their relationship as a dance. Dancing with a partner means two different entities working together. The same applies to working with existing buildings. The new construction must harmonize with its older counterpart. Both sides must somehow come together, like in our Caritas project, where we needed to reinforce the existing structure due to stability concerns. But we chose to use concrete bricks instead of mimicking the old bricks. We believe the layered history of buildings is interesting. Building, rebuilding, renovating, and reusing buildings have been ongoing practices for centuries. Why not show this?

> Flanders has a very strong building culture, especially in terms of adaptive reuse. Do you consider this a regional feature?

Absolutely. There is a saying that Belgians are born with a brick in their stomach – everyone wants a house of their own. Even young people strive for homeownership early on, often before starting a family. As many of them lack substantial funds at that life stage, they do as much as possible on their own, taking on renovations and additions themselves. Throughout Flanders you see houses with multiple self-built annexes – kitchens, bathrooms, and storage rooms – often tacked on haphazardly one behind the other. We draw inspiration from this. They may not be aesthetically perfect, but there are beautiful moments to be found in them. Ultimately, it is about people adapting existing buildings to suit their needs.

"As architects,
we have
the huge task
of changing
investors'
perspectives."

Inge Vinck

Living bricolage: Formerly a café, the Rot-Ellen-Berg house near Ghent was renovated in 2013 by De Vylder Vinck Taillieu into a private residence. Construction scaffolding and concrete formwork were integrated as permanent elements within the interior.

The result is an aesthetics reminiscent of a collage or a ready-made concept – an architecture that appears provisional yet adaptable.

I think it is essential for architects to remember that buildings have a long lifecycle. Unfortunately, this often gets overlooked in new construction projects; buildings are too quickly demolished. Instead of focusing solely on recycling individual materials, we should consider how to repurpose entire volumes and structures for different programmes. For instance: How can a parking garage be transformed into a housing block? Designs should make it easy to adapt existing buildings for new uses over time; we should look beyond rigid monofunctionality to accommodate evolving future needs.

Ghent has a rich architectural tradition. What is your favourite spot in the city?

We live in the city centre, which is where I like to be the most. I appreciate the dynamics of urban life; how people coexist. Although cities may sometimes seem less social, they provide many opportunities for social interaction and communal spaces. Ghent has a vibrant cultural scene I also enjoy. Moreover, Belgium's compact size makes it easy to explore various places – from Brussels and Antwerp to the seaside. And in the city itself, everything is within close reach, accessible by bike or on foot.

Building with Wood – but Differently

Interview
Alan Organschi

American architect Alan Organschi directs the Innovation Lab at the Bauhaus Earth research institute in Berlin. He explains to Jakob Schoof that timber construction is a way to help combat climate change – if we change how we manage forests and use wood.

Since 2021 you have been working for Bauhaus Earth, founded by climate scientist John Schellnhuber. What is this new Bauhaus – a think tank, an educational institution, a lobbying organization?

Basically all of the above. We combine research with education and outreach. Our goal is to promote ecological system change in the building sector with a broad network of actors. This is nothing fundamentally new to Europe. But our main interest is in those countries and bioregions that will experience the greatest population and consumption growth in the coming decades. This is where change in building practice will have the greatest effect.

Where do you see parallels to the historical Bauhaus?

In 1919, the aim was to deal with the consequences of World War I and to create housing for a growing middle class. The war was a catastrophe for Europe. Today we are dealing with a worldwide cataclysm, climate change. And with its enormous emissions, the building sector is in a sense the "elephant in the climate room", as John Schellnhuber puts it.

One of your focal points is timber construction. Can wood actually serve to address the global demand for new buildings to any significant extent?

Not if we carry on as we do right now. Many innovations in timber construction currently refer to the same types of wood and building products. But it would be completely wrong to use European components made of spruce or beech wood to build elsewhere in the world, to apply the capitalist logic of global trade to these resources and to overexploit regional forests for this purpose. This would only be a continuation of the previous waste of resources by other means.

What would help us instead?

We should think holistically and, at the same time, look more closely: What types of trees grow in a certain region? How can their wood be used? What regional value chains can I create by using them? And how can forests be managed in such a way that they promote biodiversity, continue to serve as CO_2 sinks, and prevent forest fires? This may sound idealistic – but given the extent to which forests are already suffering from climate change, we have little choice. By the way, we are not only concerned with building materials and their production, but also with their application: How densely and how tall do we build? How much space do we occupy – as individuals and as a communities? And, what happens at the end of the building life cycle? As long as we end up burning wood instead of reusing it, timber construction will not save us either.

Those are many questions at once. How do you approach such a Herculean task?

We look at things in a regionally differentiated way. At Bauhaus Earth, we are currently investigating four different world regions in transformation labs: Brandenburg, the Western Cape province in South Africa, Thimphu, the capital of Bhutan, and Denpasar in Indonesia. In Brandenburg, for example, we are looking at how we use wood in view of the upcoming forest transformation. We are researching the use of grasses and typha reed from paludiculture and have developed unfired masonry bricks from the gravel and clay of the gravel pits there. In Indonesia, the focus is on the use of bamboo for innovative

“As long as
we end up
burning wood
instead of
reusing it,
timber construc-
tion will not
save us either.”

Alan Organschi

An impressive structure of conjoined timber domes was designed by Gray Organschi Architecture for their carousel pavilion at Mill River Park in Stamford, Connecticut.

laminated wood products and, in the Cape Province, on ways of using eucalypt wood. In that region, eucalyptus is an invasive species that grows in large quantities. Curbing its growth makes sense in ecological terms.

And in Bhutan?

Many construction projects in the country still use concrete, mostly with cement imported from India. Yet, Bhutan is rich in forests, many of which are protected. Although timber structures are being built, the material is used very inefficiently and wood waste is not reused. Together with the forestry sector and local companies, we are now trying to diversify the product range so that more buildings can be made of wood without depleting the forests. We are also developing financing methods and working on higher energy standards for buildings, with the aim of reducing consumption here as well.

How should forests be managed in the future?

First of all, they should be managed from the get-go. If forests are left to their own devices in times of climate change, they risk turning from a CO_2 sink into a CO_2 source and start emitting greenhouse gases. Monocultures aren't the solution, either. We need increased biodiversity and crop rotation in timber plantations and commercial forests, similar to agriculture. And we must learn to use the residual wood that is collected in the course of forest maintenance.

A greater range of tree species would also result in an increased diversity of wood processing technologies. Will this lead to greater demands for research and investment?

Exactly – and this is also the reason why such ideas still encounter great resistance in the construction and timber industries.

Alan Organschi

This research station on Horse Island off the coast of Connecticut was realized through a partnership between Gray Organschi Architects and the Yale School of Architecture.

About 50% of harvested roundwood worldwide is burned for energy production. Can we allow this to continue, if we also need more and more wood for building?

I would differentiate here. Part of this amount is accounted for by private households, which take deadwood from the nearest forest and use it for heating and cooking. I find it much more critical when governments promote using wood for heating on large scales as a sustainable alternative to gas and oil. This not only causes emissions, but also lowers the pressure on us to further expand the use of other renewable energies. It also leaves us with less wood for building. I hope that this will remain a temporary phenomenon.

Craft as a Source of Energy

Interview
Anna Heringer

For Austrian architect Anna Heringer, natural building materials and local craft are pillars of sustainable architecture. To promote these more strongly in Europe, she sees the need for a new political framework, as she explains to Edeltraud Haselsteiner.

> You prefer working with clay and regionally sourced, natural building materials, and involving the local community in the development and construction process. In your work as an architect, cultural values, materials, and the local economy are therefore closely entwined.

That's right. As a 19-year-old, I had the luck to work for a development organization in Bangladesh. There I learned that the most effective strategy for resilience is to find out what resources are available on site and how to make the most of them. This concerns not only locally available materials such as clay, wood, bamboo, or straw but also local energy resources. For me, craft is the most important source of energy. It is a basic human need to be needed and to do good and meaningful work. Construction is meaningful work. It can also be beautiful work, especially when realized with natural materials. If we do not tap this source of energy, then we might also have a social problem: unemployment. Not only is there local craft, knowledge, and culture, but also global creativity and knowledge. In the past, craftspeople toured their skills, circulating their knowledge, so to speak. Later, they could apply the experiences they gained elsewhere to the conditions at home. The beauty of clay is that it can be worked purely by hand without using electricity. But it can also be processed using high-tech methods, depending on the local possibilities. The material remains the same; only the tool changes.

Anna Heringer

Do you also see a bright future for earthen construction in Europe? Labour here is relatively expensive, which makes it a significant cost factor.

That does pose a challenge, not because of the material or craft itself, but because of our economic system. If you look at craft as a form of energy, it's probably the most highly taxed. Building with local, natural building materials is always labour-intensive but mostly CO_2-neutral. It helps to counteract two of our most pressing problems: climate change and social injustice. That's why we need to do away with direct or indirect subsidies for materials such as cement, steel, aluminium, and polymers – and subsidize natural materials instead. At the very least, the true costs should be acknowledged; all the energy and CO_2 generated by the production of the material or recycling processes should be included in the calculation. Recycling concrete always leads to a loss of quality. It takes a lot of additional cement and energy for the quality to be halfway decent again. But recycled clay has the same, if not better, quality than it did before. And you only need to add water. A similar situation applies to the true cost of natural fibres. When the cheapest and most commonly used insulating materials today are petroleum-based, and natural alternatives like straw, hemp, wool, or reed are no longer affordable, then something is wrong.

What are your suggestions for establishing earthen construction better in Europe?

I imagine it working as it does in Schlins in Vorarlberg, Austria. The local clay factory produces large prefabricated elements from regional material. These are delivered stacked to the construction site, where artisanal techniques are used to build with them without additional mortar. Just as there are many local concrete mixing plants, due to limitations on how long concrete lasts in a ready mix truck, there should also be local

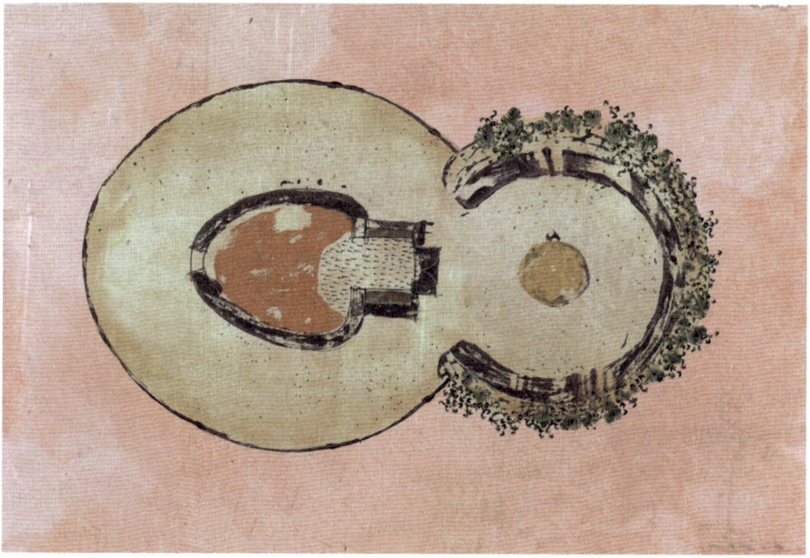

In Hittisau, a village in the Austrian state of Vorarlberg, Anna Heringer collaborated with Anka Dür, Martin Rauch, and Sabine Summer to realize this birthing room made of clay and wooden shingles.

Anna Heringer

clay factories where excavated material from each region is delivered and processed. There is abundant material available. Europe has a long tradition of earthen construction. In Germany it was used mainly for half-timbered houses, but even entire castles were built of rammed earth in Burgenland in Austria and in France. The Alhambra in Spain is also partly made of rammed earth. So the limitations exist only in our minds. Even taller earthen buildings with five to six storeys are quite feasible.

> Where else do you see a need for action in Europe to advance the use of natural building materials?

There is a need to address building codes and standards in particular, which are often influenced by the construction materials industry. There are too many liability issues, and fears are also stoked. But acting out of fear is not a good strategy. When our actions are motivated by love, towards our fellow human beings and nature, towards local construction methods and natural resources, a building becomes sustainable in a very natural way. For me, beauty is a formal, material expression of love. Beauty and good design can be leveraged to convince and inspire people.

> Energy efficiency is a major topic in the EU. How do you see it?

Energy efficiency is important, of course, but it needs to be considered in the broader context. We need to return to happy frugality. Even though we have become more technically efficient in many areas, we are still taking up more and more living space, for example – it's known as the rebound effect. This is where I see the most important leverage: when you can experience the intensity of handcrafted surfaces and healthy materials, a small space doesn't have to feel small. Together with Martin Rauch, for example, I designed relatively small

"We need to return to happy frugality. This is where I see the most important leverage."

Anna Heringer

The rooms of this Ayurveda guesthouse in Rosenheim by Anna Heringer and Martin Rauch were composed with just a few primary materials: rammed earth walls, timber, clay casein floors, and handmade ceramic tiles.

rooms of 14 to 16 m^2 at the RoSana guesthouse in Rosenheim. People accustomed to living in large rooms lived there for two weeks. But no one feels confined there because the rooms are well planned, lovingly designed, and highly refined in terms of craftsmanship. I think that is the direction we need to take, rather than trying to wrestle the problem on a high-tech level.

Anna Heringer

Creative Solutions to Combat the Climate Crisis

Interview
Sarah Wigglesworth

British architect Sarah Wigglesworth drew international attention with her Straw Bale House in London. In this interview with Heide Wessely, she describes how to design cities more sustainably.

In 2001 you built the Straw Bale House to test whether this sustainable yet unconventional building material suited to an urban context. The building won several awards but has not found many imitators. Why not?

The project was a radical departure from what was common in architecture at the time – for us, that was the incentive. We were trying to shift the debate and open up the conversation around the aesthetic issues of green architecture, which tended to be small vernacular projects in rural areas. We wanted to prove that cities can be green places as well. We rigorously decided on our material palette based around issues like embodied carbon, toxicity, pollution, and danger to people – issues that weren't common at that time. As a result, our choice of products was quite hybrid. It didn't follow the normal canon of high tech, low tech. The architectural press and profession didn't understand why we were combining these strange things altogether. For example, high-quality windows and straw bale seem to be at opposite ends of the conventional spectrum. However, the public responded really positively.
Another reason was that it's not an expensive building. It puts its money into space rather than representation. Its value system is different from most people's value systems. Most people build houses for status reasons, and they want it to look expensive, and they want it to look robust. There was also a fear of being unusual and going into the unknown realm of challenging building regulations.

Sarah Wigglesworth

The Straw Bale House, built by Sarah Wigglesworth Architects in 2001, was renovated in 2021 to enhance accessibility for ageing residents and improve energy efficiency while maintaining its unique appearance.

So clients aren't brave enough to have railroad ties used as window lintels, straw insulation, and walls made out of sandbags?

Exactly. Where do these materials sit in the value system? When we built the building, it didn't have much currency in the value system. Luckily, things have changed a bit. There is more awareness that we're very wasteful as a society. I'm not suggesting that bales are now mainstream, but I think everybody is now much, much more aware of issues such as recycling, the circular economy, and repurposing existing buildings. Renewable building materials that sequester carbon instead of emitting it are also gaining in importance, such as hemp. You can use it to weave carpets, but also build entire houses with it. When combined with lime, it becomes so strong that it can even be used for foundations. In France, there are about 600 buildings made out of hemp; in the UK, there are only about 25. I think it really needs to get more on the map.

Why has it been so hard for the industry to adopt sustainable construction methods and renewable materials? The UN's 2020 Global Status Report for Buildings and Construction revealed that global CO_2 emissions are at record levels – and the construction sector is responsible for 38 % of that.

I'm baffled that it hasn't gotten more purchase with the construction industry because it's just such an obvious thing that we have to address. I think construction is risk-averse and monopolistic. Perhaps there are too many in the industry who are comfortable doing what they do.

What needs to change?

I think legislation is the answer. We need people committed to this agenda, who will invest more in new processes, new collection systems, rainwater drainage systems, alternative energy sources, new materials that are part of a circular economy etc. It's not happening at the grassroots level. Of course, there are some exceptions, but I think, on the whole, people are not innovating enough, and they're not addressing this problem out of their own moral compass. Everybody is waiting for someone else to make a move because they don't want to be the one who will suffer from having to invest more in new processes or techniques that might not pay off in the end. By only waiting and watching, the situation gets worse – it's a big loop that is very difficult to disrupt. The problem is that time is not on our side.

What can architects do about it?

Everybody has to do something, every one of us. We have to ask ourselves: Is it sustainable how we live, travel, shop, and eat? All these things present us with an ethical dilemma. It's hard, but I think we have to make changes in nearly every part of our lives. As architects, we can influence opinion: of our clients, manufacturers, and policymakers. Our practice is small, but we have been working on sustainability in architecture for 25 years and have achieved quite a bit. We have produced low-energy schools and housing and are retrofitting old housing stock – a lot of which is social housing – to improve their environmental performance. It's not very sexy work, but it's very important work.

The construction industry accounts for around 55 % of materials consumption; only 1 % is reused. We seldom hear about that. On the other hand, there are loud calls to ban disposable cups and drinking straws. Does that make sense?

In the face of something that is as big as climate change, it's very difficult for individuals to work out: What can I do? What

"As architects, we can influence opinion: of our clients, manufacturers, and policymakers."

Sarah Wigglesworth

can help? That is part of the dilemma. Doing without plastic cups is a small thing, but it's a tiny thing that somebody can do easily. Shifting the construction industry is a huge issue that I can't do anything about. But the plastic cup is a route into understanding your part in the bigger picture, which is good: it raises awareness.

How can we make our cities more sustainable?

One thing would be to ban cars from cities, and everyone should ride a bicycle. Then you should change the public realm so that all streets have trees and create sponge cities to cope with rainwater drainage. I would make all buildings out of cross-laminated timber to replace concrete completely. Although we need high density in the cities, I would not build tower blocks because they are wasteful and use a lot of energy because the transportation is vertical. To live a healthy life, we should be walking, cycling, using the stairs, and seeing our neighbours more often – all the things that make us feel good. Inclusion and diversity also are very important in architecture; there are currently different groups of people who feel quite excluded by the way we design the built environment.

Your vision reminds me of the 15-minute city, where you can reach all essential facilities in 15 minutes by bike or on foot. In reality, it usually takes longer to get to work.

Most cities have been planned around men's journeys and the idea that women stay at home in the suburbs and men travel into town to their offices or factories. It's a crazy notion, yet cities cement that into the way we live. We need to get away from that and support more sustainable ways of living. Vienna has an interesting approach: every urban planning project must be assessed as to how it will affect women's lives. Their journey patterns tend to be very different from men's. Women often

Sarah Wigglesworth Architects transformed a disused Victorian-era school building in South London into the Siobhan Davies Dance Studios, creating a bright space for creative movement.

Sarah Wigglesworth

The Bike & Ride Station at Kingston Station in London features a three-story bicycle parking hub, a pedestrian bridge, and a recreational park along the train tracks.

do most of the housework, do the shopping, drop the kids at school, go to work, and care for their elders. What we design impacts women's lives. So far, they have effectively been ignored, and a mind shift is required to make things easier for them.

That sounds like a clear case of discrimination.

Women are still not equal; but if we manage to give more weight to women with their experiences and the way they live, we might get a more equal and more sustainable society.

Potential of Clay Archi tecture

Interview
Roger Boltshauser

Boltshauser Architects won the Detail Award 2022 for its kiln tower for a brickworks museum in Switzerland. Swiss architect Roger Boltshauser has also designed larger rammed earth buildings – and observes growing enthusiasm among clients for this natural material, as he reveals to Jakob Schoof.

The kiln tower in Cham, which you designed with students from TU Munich, is apparently the world's first building made of prestressed rammed earth. How did it come about?

The museum is on the site of an old brickyard, which included a customary clay pit. The management wanted to show what was possible with this material and asked if we could design a rammed earth building for the museum grounds. At the same time, it had to be a temporary structure because it was not located in a designated building area. The idea of prestressing rammed earth was born in 2016–17 while I was a visiting professor at EPFL in Lausanne. A student designed a prestressed clay-wood ceiling and produced it as a mockup. The prestressing allowed the slab to withstand bending loads. Rammed earth alone can only absorb compressive forces. We then turned the concept vertically and developed it further with engineer Jürg Conzett. First, we produced a large facade mockup in 2019 at the Sitterwerk in St. Gallen, followed by the kiln tower in Cham.

What are the advantages of prestressing, and what factors must be considered?

You can build higher, slimmer walls in particular. In Cham, the rammed earth walls are nearly 10 metres high. Without prestressing, they could only be 5 to 6 metres high at most. The wall construction – large, prefabricated elements with all the joints visible between them – would hardly have been possible without the prestressing. One challenge in prestressed

Roger Boltshauser

earthen construction is creep and shrinkage: the clay contracts over time and the prestressing tendons loosen. So for the kiln tower, we used prefabricated rammed earth blocks that were allowed to dry for almost a year before installation to reduce shrinkage. We also integrated steel springs into the prestressing steel to keep constant high pressure on the outer walls. We are now measuring whether this method works over the long term and if it is suitable for larger construction projects.

Particularly in Switzerland, research is being conducted into innovative clay structures. What are some promising approaches?

At ETH Zurich, Guillaume Habert is researching liquid clay mixtures that can be poured like concrete into formwork. This usually requires additives like plasticizers and hardeners. So it is not as recyclable as our kiln tower but is still almost 100 % clay. There are also attempts to stabilize clay structures by adding binders like lime or cement. Students at ETH Zurich have rammed reinforcing cages into clay walls, quadrupling the compressive load that the clay can carry. It requires different reinforcements than concrete ones, and development is still in its early stages, but it could be a promising approach. In general, we think the future belongs to intelligent hybrid structures made of clay with wood, steel, or concrete. And it does not always have to be rammed earth. For example, one of the largest brickworks in Switzerland is considering producing unfired bricks in response to the energy crisis this winter. Technically, it would not be a big change for them.

For design reasons, many architects want to leave rammed earth visible. How does that square with today's insulation codes?

There are different methods. You can have a double-skin facade with core insulation or insulate the clay walls from the

The kiln tower for the Ziegelei Museum in Cham, Switzerland, designed and built by ETH Zurich students in collaboration with Roger Boltshauser, is the world's first prestressed clay building – a built experiment.

Roger Boltshauser

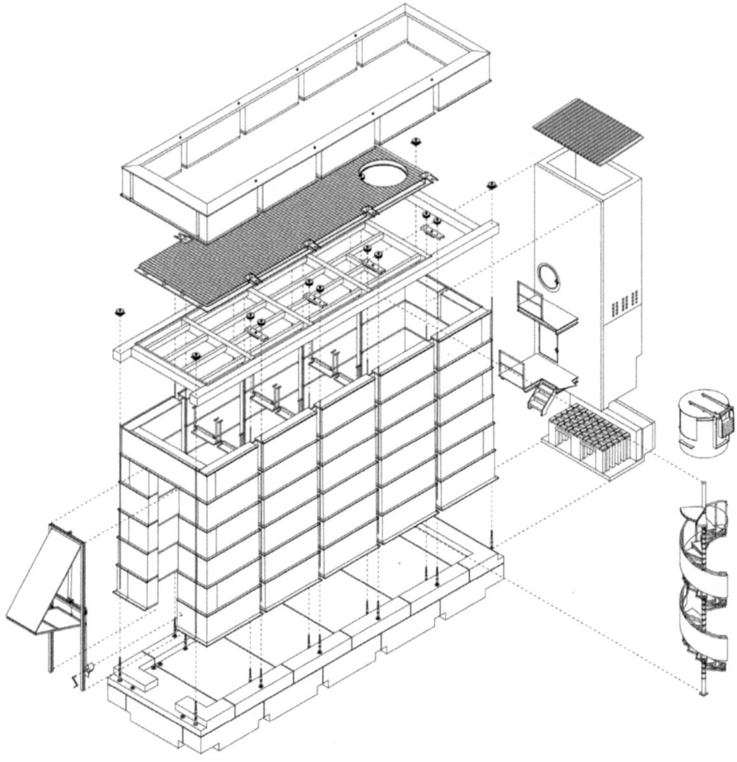

Six rows of prefabricated rammed earth elements form the outer walls of the kiln tower. They are dry stacked, making them easy to disassemble.

inside. Even on its own, clay achieves a significantly better U-value than concrete and brick. We are researching mixtures with even higher insulating properties, for instance, by adding chopped corn to the clay. In Switzerland, most historic earthen buildings are plastered. Lime plaster protects the clay from the elements and covers any insulation installed on the facade. Perhaps architects should put vanity aside when it comes to the carbon footprint.

How is client acceptance of earthen architecture?

Despite being associated with earthen architecture, we have seldom been able to build with the material in the last 20 years. We often proposed earthen buildings in our competition designs, which were first met with enthusiasm by the juries and later clients. But that was followed by lengthy discussions, and the idea was eventually dropped. Clients had too many doubts about the supposedly novel material, it was too expensive, or they were worried that the walls would erode. But recently, it seems that the climate and energy crisis has fostered a new sense of openness. We are currently working on a large sports centre in Zurich-Oerlikon with 25 metre-high rammed earth stair towers, in which we will integrate large hot water tanks. The city is proud of the project, and those responsible for the project want it. Of course, they ask how it all works, and sometimes the old fears come up when signing contracts. But I am confident that we will see a growing number of larger earthen buildings in the future.

Many of your designs involve thermally activated clay building elements or large water tanks for solar heat. Do you have a standard approach to building technology?

In general, the more passive, the better. This makes it possible to achieve a great deal, even with technically complex buildings. Thanks to large heat tanks, the pool in Oerlikon is entirely independent from district heating. And with a photovoltaic system integrated into the facade, we produce most of the electricity we need ourselves. But building services cannot be wholly eliminated. As architects, we must develop solutions for today's tasks, finding the optimal balance between low energy costs, low CO_2 emissions, and the lowest possible use of technology.

"I am confident that we will see a growing number of larger earthen buildings in the future."

Roger Boltshauser

Appendix

Conversation Partners

41 Kunlé Adeyemi

71 Shigeru Ban

21 Tatiana Bilbao

211 Roger Boltshauser

153 Michael Braungart

109 Barbara Buser

143 Catherine De Wolf

81 Richard Hassell

189 Anna Heringer

[13] Lacol

[13] Anders Lendager

[13] Lamia Messari-Becker

[179] Alan Organschi

[33] Tarik Oualalou

[99] Michael Pawlyn

[11] Marina Tabassum

[51] Camilla van Deurs

[169] Inge Vinck

[89] Richard Weller

[199] Sarah Wigglesworth

Conversation Partners

41 **Kunlé Adeyemi** is a Nigerian architect. He studied at the University of Lagos and Princeton University School of Architecture, New Jersey. Before starting his practice for architecture, design, and urbanism in Amsterdam in 2010, he worked for nearly a decade at OMA. He has taught and given lectures at universities worldwide.

71 **Shigeru Ban** is mostly known for his buildings consisting of paper as a construction material. The atypical use of materials is a characteristic of many of his buildings. He founded the Voluntary Architects' Network (VAN) in order to support communities impacted by catastrophic events. In 2014 he was awarded the Pritzker prize.

21 **Tatiana Bilbao** founded her practice in Mexico City in 2004. With her team, she designs buildings and masterplans that specifically address people and their environment. Bilbao has years of expertise in social housing. Her projects reflect a sense of simplicity and stringency.

211 **Roger Boltshauser** heads Boltshauser Architekten in Zurich and Munich. Earthen architecture has long been a focus of his research and teaching. He is currently also a lecturer at ETH Zurich.

153 **Michael Braungart** is a process engineer with a doctorate in chemistry. In collaboration with William McDonough, he developed the cradle-to-cradle (C2C) concept in the 1990s. Braungart is the founder and director of the Hamburg-based Environmental Protection Encouragement Agency (EPEA), an institute that assists corporations in integrating circular processes into their value chains. Since 2008, he has held the Cradle-to-Cradle professorship at Erasmus University Rotterdam and serves as a professor of Eco-Design at Leuphana University of Lüneburg.

109 **Barbara Buser** graduated in architecture from ETH Zurich in 1979 and then worked in Africa for 10 years. In 1996, she and Klara Kläusler founded the first-ever Bauteilbörse (building parts exchange) in Basel. Together withEric Honegger she has initiated and realized numerous conversion projects. At the 2021 Venice Architecture Biennale, her practice Baubüro in situ received the Global Gold Award from the Holcim Foundation for Sustainable Construction for the K.118 project in Winterthur.

143 **Catherine De Wolf** is an assistant professor at ETH Zurich, where she heads the Chair of Circular Engineering for Architecture (CEA). She is a faculty member at the Center for Augmented Computational Design in Architecture, Engineering and Construction (Design ++), the ETH AI Center, and the National Competence Center of Research on Digital Fabrication. She cofounded the Digital Circular Economy (DiCE) Lab and the circular construction company Anku.

89 **Richard Hassell,** a native Australian, founded WOHA with Wong Mun Summ in 1994. The Singapore-based practice focuses on conceiving integrated architectural and urban design solutions to tackle the problems of the 21st century, such as climate change, population growth, and rapidly increasing urbanization.

189 **Anna Heringer** studied architecture in Linz and won international acclaim with her final project, the Meti Handmade School in Bangladesh. She designs sustainable buildings worldwide, using locally sourced materials. Heringer is the recipient of the New European Bauhaus Award and the Aga Khan Award for Architecture, among others.

61 **Lacol** is an architecture cooperative founded in 2009 while its members were still university students. Eliseu Arrufat and Carles Baiges represent the collective of 13 members. Lacol is best known for its cooperative apartment buildings, which have gained international recognition and acclaim.

121 **Anders Lendager** is an architect and CEO and founder of the Lendager Group in Copenhagen, which comprises an architectural practice as well as a business consultancy focusing on recycled building materials. Lendager also advises the United Nations on the implementation of the Sustainable Development Goals and is a visiting professor at Aarhus University.

133 **Lamia Messari-Becker,** professor for Building Technology and Building Physics at University of Siegen, holds a PhD in civil engineering and was partner and director of an engineering firm. She is a key climate expert in committees like Germany's Expert Panel on Future Construction and the Club of Rome. Since 2024, she has been State Secretary of the Hessian Ministry for Economic Affairs, Energy, Transport, Housing and Rural Development.

179 **Alan Organschi** heads the architectural practice Gray Organschi Architecture in New Haven, Connecticut, together with Elizabeth Gray and teaches at the Yale School of Architecture. In 2021 he was named director of the Innovation Lab at Bauhaus Earth in Potsdam.

33 **Tarik Oualalou** is founding partner of the architecture firm Oualalou + Choi , based in Paris and Casablanca. A native of the Moroccan capital of Rabat, he studied architecture and civil engineering in Paris, worked for architecture firms in the USA, and has taught at universities in the USA, France, and Morocco for around 20 years.

99 **Michael Pawlyn** is cofounder of Architects Declare, an architect, and pioneer of biomimetic architecture and regenerative design. His practice, Exploration Architecture, implements progressive projects at a wide range of scales. He is a frequent keynote speaker and author of "Biomimicry in Architecture" and co-author with Sarah Ichioka of "Flourish: Design Paradigms for Our Planetary Emergency".

11 **Marina Tabassum** established her practice in Dhaka, Bangladesh, in 2005 after ten years as partner and cofounder of Urbana. Through work spanning institutional buildings, apartment buildings, and cultural institutions, Marina Tabassum Architects (MTA) seeks to establish an architectural language that is contemporary yet reflectively rooted in place.

51 **Camilla van Deurs** was a partner at Gehl Architects before becoming Copenhagen's Chief City Architect in 2019. Her goal is to make cities even more liveable and sustainable. With a PhD in Urban Design, she has been a driving force in numerous green initiatives. She chairs Copenhagen's involvement in CirCuit, a collaborative EU project focusing on circular construction in regenerative cities.

169 **Inge Vinck** cofounded architecten Jan de Vylder Inge Vinck in Ghent and teaches at Kunst Akademie Düsseldorf. Vinck views architecture as more of a mandate, not only a service. Currently, she and her team are working on the adaptive reuse of Palais des Expositions in Charleroi, Belgium, and the design of a high-rise housing block in Switzerland. These projects prioritize material conservation and concrete as a building component.

89 **Richard Weller** is the Meyerson Chair of Urbanism and Professor of Landscape Architecture at the University of Pennsylvania in Philadelphia. His research focuses on the conflicts between biodiversity and urban growth, leading to initiatives such as the World Park Project as well as the web-based Hotspot Cities Project and Atlas for the End of the World.

199 **Sarah Wigglesworth** founded her practice in London in 1994. Most of her team are women. Increasing women's presence in architecture is one of the award-winning architect's priorities. She also focuses on the participation of users and clients in the design process, interdisciplinary planning, especially for cities, and sustainable construction.

Authors

Vera Simone Bader earned her doctorate in art history from Humboldt University in Berlin. Since 2013, she has worked at Architekturmuseum München, curating various exhibitions. Additionally, she serves as a research assistant at the Chair of Architectural History and Curatorial Practice at the Technical University of Munich.

Jan D. Geipel worked after studying architecture in Stuttgart and Copenhagen for C.F. Møller, Riken Yamamoto, and Vitra. From 2009 to 2012, he curated exhibitions and conferences at the Danish Architecture Center (DAC) in Copenhagen. Until 2017, he served as Dean of Interior and Space Design at the University of Art and Design (HEAD) in Geneva.

Edeltraud Haselsteiner works as a project manager, researcher, exhibition curator, and architecture journalist with a focus on sustainable architecture, urban planning, and mobility. She founded the Urbanity Research Institute and has taught at various universities (Vienna University of Technology, University of Applied Arts Vienna, University of Klagenfurt). She has edited numerous specialized architecture publications.

Sandra Hofmeister studied architecture and art history in Berlin and earned a doctorate in Romance studies from Ludwig-Maximilians-Universität Munich. Editor-in-chief of Detail from 2016 to January 2025, she now works as an architecture critic, moderator, and juror for international competitions. She is also committed to promoting architectural book culture through the castello books platform.

Frank Kaltenbach has been a member of the Detail editorial team since 1998. He studied architecture at the University of Stuttgart and Arizona State University in Phoenix (USA). He has worked as an architect in Tokyo, Vienna, and Munich. He also teaches the history of architecture and design at the Academy of Fine Arts in Munich.

Julia Liese studied architecture and urban planning at the University of Stuttgart and Tampere University of Technology in Finland. Her passion for writing emerged during her studies, leading to her first journalistic experiences. Following a traineeship at Detail, she has been serving as an editor since 2006, overseeing various magazines and contributing to several books in this capacity.

Peter Popp joined the Detail editorial team in 2001. He studied architecture at the Technical University of Munich and the Technical University of Darmstadt, and pursued journalism at the Institute for Journalism and Communication Research in Hanover. At Detail, he has produced architectural films for the online portal and coordinates editorial content. He also shares his expertise as a lecturer in architectural theory at the Technical University of Nuremberg.

Jakob Schoof, the deputy editor-in-chief of Detail, has spent nearly 25 years sharing architectural knowledge. After graduating in architecture from the University of Karlsruhe in 2000, he worked at the architecture magazine AIT, first as an intern, then editor, and later head of corporate publishing. Joining Detail in 2009, his projects have included overseeing Detail Green, a magazine and book series on sustainable construction, and the structural design magazine Structure.

Heide Wessely studied architecture in Munich and London. Her British diploma enabled her to work in Hong Kong, where she first worked with a graphic designer and later in an architecture firm. Upon returning to Germany, she spent five years as an employed architect, focusing on planning laboratory and university buildings, before joining Detail as an editor in 1999. She dedicated a sabbatical and other free time to designing and constructing small social projects in Sri Lanka and Uganda. Since 2024, she has been living and working in her second adopted home, Barcelona.

Barbara Zettel moved to Southeast Asia after completing her studies in Regensburg, living in Surabaya and Singapore for eleven years. During this time, she worked in various aspects of architecture, including residential construction and exhibition design. For the German European School Singapore, she developed a curriculum for teaching architecture as part of the polytechnic curriculum. Upon returning to Munich, her passion for impactful architecture led her to Detail, where she has served as an editor since 2018.

Authors

Images

16, 18 Asif Salman
26, 29, 30 Estudio Tatiana Bilbao
37 Oualalou + Choi
44 Kriolscope
46 Kunlé Adeyemi
49 Iwan Baan
54 Visit Copenhagen/ Martin Heiberg
57 Cycle Superhighways/ Capital region of Denmark
58 City of Copenhagen, TU-data
66 Álvaro Valdecantos
69 City of Barcelona
75 Hiroyuki Hirai
76 Shigeru Ban Architects/ Voluntary Architects' Network
87 Patrick Bingham-Hall
93 Richard Weller
104 Claudia Härterich, Hauke Hartmann, Thieß Petersen, Geteilte Verantwortung beim globalen Klimaschutz, Bertelsmann Stiftung, October 2021
113, 116, 119 baubüro in situ ag / Martin Zeller
125↑, 126↑ Rasmus Hjortshøj
125↓, 126↓, 131 Lendager Architects
138↑ Lucas van der Wee
138↓ cepezed
141 Stefan Forster Architekten
149, 150 Buser, Hill
158 Ossip van Duivenbode
161 Brigida González
162 Nikolai Brenner
173, 176 Filip Dujardin
184 David Sundberg/ Esto
186 Millie Yoshida
193↑ Laurenz Feinig
193↓ Studio Anna Heringer
196 Gabrical
202 Paul Smoothy
207 Peter Cook
208 Buro Happold
215 Kuster Frey
216 Boltshauser Architects
222 Photo Kunlé Adeyemi: Mark Horn

222 Photo Shigeru Ban: Shigeru Ban Architects
222 Photo Tatiana Bilbao: Luis Garvan
222 Photo Roger Boltshauser: Michael Artur Koenig
222 Photo Michael Braungart: Raphael Gabauer
222 Photo Barbara Buser: baubüro in situ ag/Martin Zeller
222 Photo Catherine De Wolf: Nicole Davidson
222 Photo Richard Hassell: Studio Periphery
222 Photo Anna Heringer: Gerald von Foris
223 Photo Lacol: Lacol
223 Photo Anders Lendager: Mikkel Hvilshøj
223 Photo Lamia Messari-Becker: Judith Schmitz
223 Photo Alan Organschi: Gray Organschi Architecture
223 Photo Tarik Oualalou: Oualalou + Choi
223 Photo Michael Pawlyn: ajdviv
223 Photo Marina Tabassum: Sounak Das
223 Photo Camilla van Deurs: Camilla van Deurs
223 Photo Inge Vinck: Inge Vinck
223 Photo Richard Weller: Richard Weller
223 Photo Sarah Wigglesworth: Jim Stephenson

Imprint

Editor
Dr. Sandra Hofmeister

Interviewers
Vera Simone Bader, Jan D. Geipel, Edeltraud Haselsteiner, Sandra Hofmeister, Frank Kaltenbach, Julia Liese, Peter Popp, Jakob Schoof, Heide Wessely, Barbara Zettel

Project Management
Edith Walter

Editorial Support
Laura Traub

Translations
Alisa Kotmair,
Mark Kammerbauer

Proofreading
Alisa Kotmair

Design
Claudia Scheer, Manuel Federl (Berlin, DE)
→ muskat.design

DTP
Simone Soesters

Reproduction
ludwig:media (Zell am See, AT)
→ ludwigmedia.at

Printing and Binding
Gutenberg Beuys Feindruckerei (Langenhagen, DE)
→ feindruckerei.de

Paper
Cover: Chromosulfate cardboard 280 g
Content: Munken Print White 100 g

This book has been made from materials that originate from responsibly managed, FSC®-certified forests and other verified sustainable sources.

FSC www.fsc.org MIX Paper | Supporting responsible forestry FSC® C009051

DETAIL Architecture
GmbH (Munich, DE)
→ detail.de
→ books@detail.de

ISBN:
978-3-95553-628-2 (Print)
978-3-95553-629-9 (E-Book)

«No hay mejor regalo que se pueda dar a otra persona que enseñarle a conocer a Dios y ser conocido por él. En *Quédate quieto*, Brian Heasley nos ofrece ese regalo. Brian es un hombre que se sienta a los pies de Jesús, y en estas páginas, tú también querrás sentarte allí junto a él».

TYLER STATON
Director nacional de *Oración 24-7 EE. UU.*

«Este libro describe la dirección que me gustaría tomar en mi vida de oración. El autor nos recuerda que no hay una sola manera de orar, sino muchas, y que podemos escuchar nuestra propia mente y corazón para discernir cuál es la mejor para nosotros en este momento. Como ya estoy en la tercera edad, aprecié mucho su recordatorio de que Dios nos sorprende con cosas nuevas en cada etapa de la vida. ¡Es tan cierto!».

ALICE FRYLING
Directora espiritual y autora de *Aging Faithfully: The Holy Invitation of Growing Older* (Envejecer fielmente: La santa invitación a envejecer)

«Un marco práctico y de vital importancia para enriquecer esta disciplina diaria».

MARK SAYERS
Autor de *A Non-Anxious Presence: How a Changing and Complex World Will Create a Remnant of Renewed Christian Leaders* (Una presencia sin ansiedad: Cómo un mundo cambiante y complejo creará un remanente de líderes cristianos renovados)

«Ya sea que tengas experiencia en el hábito diario del "tiempo devocional" con Dios, o estés recién comenzando o buscando un refrigerio, te recomiendo este hermoso libro de todo corazón. Esta guía ingeniosa, vulnerable, totalmente práctica, rica y creativa ayudará a todo buscador genuino de Dios».

REVERENDA SOPHIE JELLEY
Obispa de Doncaster